THE KURDISH GIRL

A NOVEL

By Lone Bendixen Goulani

ISBN: 9788740454123
Cover design: Esben Dam
Graphic design: Ole Sejrup Jensen and Gitte Bendixen
Printed in Germany

Preface

Once upon a time, there was an old Kurdish man who decided to give his sons their inheritance while he was still alive. He owned a lot of land, which he asked his sons to divide amongst themselves, and also a blue donkey which he wished to sell in order to use the money to remarry since he was a widower. The sons immediately started to quarrel about who should have what piece of land. One wanted a certain slot of land and another strongly disagreed, and this discussion went on, and on, and on until the old man interrupted their conversation.

"What about the blue donkey?" he asked. "When are we going to talk about the blue donkey?"

The Wedding Night

It was a clear November day. The chairs in Havana Star Wedding Hall were decorated with thin, white cloth and on the tables stood plates with salted mixed nuts and kernels, a plate of fruit, and a box of Kleenex. The guests (most of them from Hewler and the village of Banaman, just outside the Kurdish capital) were waiting patiently for the bride and groom to appear, so the party could start. Cameras on little cranes were already running, and on a huge widescreen, women could see and judge each other's dresses, hair, makeup, and amount of jewellery. Every woman was trying to shimmer more than the others. The gossip had started with the delivery of the wedding invitations. An old woman, called Baji, clad in a Kurdish black dress sparsely decorated with small crystals, started the conversation at her table by asking into the air:

"Who is this girl Shiawa that Kak Bahrus has married? I've never heard about her family."

"Her father is a martyr," a plump woman in a traditional purple dress with lots of crystals said. "Apparently, he passed away during Saddam Hussein's regime when she was very little."

"Did her mother remarry?" Baji raised her eyebrows.

"No, and the girl does not have any sisters or brothers," the woman in purple answered.

"Oh, poor girl."

"I heard her mother got a sewing machine from a Dutch organisation. She is sewing for people," the woman in purple continued.

"I see," Baji said.

"At least they get the martyr pension and the rations. That is not bad after all."

"Not bad at all," Baji repeated.

"That is why she is so skinny. Look at my daughter," the plump lady said and pointed at a girl with fat arms and rosy apple cheeks sitting with a group of other young girls. "This is how a bride should look."

"Mashallah, she is certainly beautiful." Baji said but quickly returned to talk more about the couple: "Poor Kak Bahrus' parents! Why did he not discuss this matter with them before he asked for her hand?"

The woman in the purple dress started to rearrange her heavy gold necklace but nodded to Baji.

"Aye, this is the modern disrespectful way of entering a marriage – and this is even his second wife! I guess it is because the first one could not give him any babies, but is he really that rich?" Baji asked.

"I think so. His father owns the K Energy Petrol station and, he has several greenhouses, but still…"

The music got so loud that nobody could hear what the women said, and Bahrus stepped onto the red carpet. He walked up the aisle, greeting people on both sides, clapping his chest and saluting other men. He stopped in front of the little podium with massive plastic flower decorations, burning candles and two big heavy armchairs where he was going to sit with his new wife the rest of the evening. He dabbed his forehead with a Kleenex, and shifted from one foot to the other, looking at everybody and nobody at the same time. Where the women looked suspicious, the men smiled at him. The women pitied his first wife Lara, but the men envied Bahrus, yet would naturally keep quiet about that to satisfy their own wives.

Then Shiawa came, and immediately people around her started to clap, ululate and sing. She looked beautiful in her puffy white wedding dress, with bare shoulders, and over her big almond shaped eyes, lots of purple and black eye makeup that was visible to everyone because she stared at her tiny wrists and long fingers and did not dare to look at anybody. Fireworks started to sprout along the red carpet, and the nearest bystanders screamed and took a few steps back. Finally, she reached Bahrus. He took her hands, kissed her on her forehead, then grabbed her around her waist and they started to dance a slow dance to Celine Dion's "My Heart Will Go On" since it was her favourite song. A deep sigh went through the audience. Most people stared at the dancing couple and acted as if this was a totally normal wedding party procedure, but people like the fat lady in the purple dress and Baji looked at each other with a slightly open mouth and raised eyebrows.

When Shiawa and Bahrus sat down in the armchairs, the Havana band took over, and the Kurdish music started. People flocked to the dance floor, and long chains of people, holding hands, shoulder to shoulder, started to dance to the Kurdish rhythms by lifting one foot and putting it down next to the other again and again and again while lifting their shoulders up and down. The fun had begun.

Najeeba was standing close by and watched her daughter. What a grand party it was. She was familiar with the gossip concerning her daughter's marriage. She had asked Shiawa what she would do in case Bahrus ever wanted to remarry in case she could not get pregnant, and since Shiawa expressed an understanding for a man's wish to become a father, she did not say more. It was also Bahrus' duty to inform Shiawa about his first wife anyway. She had decided not to interfere with her daughter's love. Frankly, she was afraid Shiawa (with her twenty-six years of age) was getting too old to ever find a husband. Any marriage was a blessing. Fortunately, Bahrus was only thirty, and he had promised her that he no longer loved his first wife since she had turned grim and bitter after not being able to get pregnant, and she did take care of all the housework in the house, so Shiawa would be able to focus on her studies. Najeeba was not sure it would all be perfect, but after all, no marriage was, and so she let her daughter dream on and did not share her worries. Nobody ever wanted to be the devil's tongue and least of all her. The only thing she wanted was for her daughter to be happy, and she did not want to ruin everything by her negative thinking. She caught her daughter's eye and they both smiled.

Shiawa had packed her new suitcase months and months ago. Now it was waiting for her in Uncle Ahmed's old pickup outside in the parking lot, waiting for her to unzip it and lead a new life in Banaman. It still made her frown a little to think that her new life was going to be in the little village at the foot of the mountain, and not above, in the bigger town of Masif Sallahadin, overlooking all the lights from the capital. Bahrus had told everybody that he lived in Masif Sallahadin when he had introduced himself to their classmates at Hewler Agricultural College, but her uncle had informed her that this was not the case. Her uncle was like a father to her. He was only young when Shiawa's father passed away, and since her father did not have any brothers to take care of her and her mother, Uncle Ahmed had taken this responsibility on himself. She would always love him for taking care of them. Perhaps Bahrus told people he lived in Masif because he assumed, they would not know about such a small village even though the Khanzad castle once was inhabited by a Kurdish princess and was quite a famous landmark in Kurdistan. Another thing was that his parents lived in Masif Sallahadin and apparently owned a lot of land in addition to the K Energy Petrol station. Anyway, she was getting married, and that was the most important thing.

Bahrus had set up three big green houses in Banaman a few years back where he grew all sorts of herbs and vegetables. He was popular at college for this agricultural success, and everybody wanted to know how much he had invested, and what the yearly outcome was. Bahrus' brother oversaw the family's vegetable shop in the bazaar just opposite the old mosque where he sold Bahrus' vegetables at very high prices to the rich Barzani families who never asked about the prices. Things were going well for the family.

From her armchair, Shiawa watched people dance and admired the women's traditional dresses. In her suitcase, laid ten brand new Kurdish dresses that her mother had patiently sewn for her during the cold winter months. There were also cotton nightgowns for summer, velvet night gowns for winter, underwear, sandals, perfume, makeup, and a lot of other items that every newlywed wife needed. Everything was unused and had been selected under close consultation with her mother. She loved her mother so much. Tears pressed behind her eyelids. How could she live without her mother from tonight and onwards? How could she leave her mother in their little house where they had shared so many cold winter nights by the kerosene heater, so many hot summer days sleeping the afternoons lazily away before waking up to eat watermelon and watch the Korean series on television?

She pushed the thoughts away as a small family with three little kids stepped onto the little podium to have their photo taken with them. The kids looked beautiful in their mini Kurdish outfits, but she did not know who they were. It would be inappropriate to smile, and they all stared motionless into the camera, the photographer shot the photo, and the cameraman got everything on tape. The family went down and now a long line of people was waiting to have a photo shot with them, and she smiled and enjoyed the attention.

Bahrus' mother went around to the tables with a huge tray to collect gold from the guests.

"Congratulations, Mother of Kak Bahrus!"

"Inshallah, may they live long."

"Mashallah, your daughter-in-law is very beautiful. May Allah protect her."

The tray got heavier and heavier, and she finally made her way to the couple. She took out the present for her new daughter-in-law – a heavy necklace which she put around Shiawa's neck, followed by kisses on her cheeks. The camera zoomed in on the necklace and everybody in the hall was able to admire the big – and obviously very expensive – present on the big screens. Shiawa felt very happy. Her mother-in-law was sweet and in addition showed it to everybody.

After another hour, the wedding cake was brought in by the servants, who also brought a huge sword decorated with a pink ribbon. She and Bahrus got up and laid their hands on the sword, posed for the camera and cut the cake. He took a little spoonful of cake and fed her, and she did the same. The cameras went "click, click, click" everywhere around them. Only the top layer was a cake. The rest of it was just made with boxes and decorated with cream. They looked at each other and smiled, and Bahrus secretly touched her hand. They sat down again, the music continued, and Bahrus' brother took the sword and danced around with it cutting dangerously into the air.

The young girls danced and stared at each other trying to look as respectable as possible, while at the same time announcing their availability to enter marriage. Two brave young men from Banaman finally decided to break the girl's chain, and as they were both good looking and had chosen to hold hands with Banaman's two most popular and beautiful girls, a lot of tension suddenly started to build up on the dance floor. The girls pretended they were not boiling over by the touch of a man, and luckily the huge amount of foundation covered the red spots on their necks and cheeks. The Kurdish chain dance got wilder and wilder, and some of Bahrus' cousins from Banaman were sweating heavily from jumping up and down, apparently in some sort of trance.

Only few people noticed that Shiawa and Bahrus left the party while most people were dancing. Bahrus' brother drove them back to Banaman after getting Shiawa's suitcase from her uncle's pickup. He drove their parent's car –a luxurious Toyota Land Cruiser decorated with pink ribbons, plastic flowers and fluffy material. His father had bought it through a businessman who often went to Baghdad. It was used and had only cost nine thousand dollars, but it had been bloodstained, and there were still bullet holes in the windshield. The moon was nearly full, and the sky was dark grey, lighting up the mountain they drove towards. Only a single star shone. Once they got closer, she could see the Khanzad castle, and she started to feel nervous about the expectations for their first night together. Everybody had so many expectations about everything. She was wondering how she was ever going to fulfil them. They arrived to Banaman, and the Land Cruiser easily drove up the driveway, which was lit with green, blue, and red garden lamps, and the shadows of the trees and bushes welcomed her. The village was quiet since most of the villagers were in Havana Star Hall celebrating their marriage, but still everywhere lights were lit. They got out of the car, and Bahrus' brother took her suitcase and put it in the hall. He said goodbye to Bahrus but avoided her look. After all, it was an awkward situation to be in. Bahrus took her hand and led her upstairs. There was a strange smell in the house of deodorising balls for the toilet, fresh paint and kerosene. Not unpleasant, but a new smell she would have to get used to. Bahrus opened the door to the bedroom and switched on the lights.

"Oh Bahrus, it's so beautiful!" Shiawa let out a deep sigh.

They had selected the bedroom furniture together on the Sixty Meter Road. The dark wood look-a-like material made the room look even smaller than it was, but little crystals on the handles, a huge mirror on the wardrobe, and a synthetic bedspread with organza flowers and lots of little shiny beads mirrors, and pearls lit it all up.

"It's worthy of a princess," Bahrus said and turned on the heaters in the cold room.

Then he went outside for a smoke to give Shiawa a chance to change her clothes. She heard him speaking on the phone, but she could not hear exactly what he said. From her suitcase on the floor, she got out a white satin night gown which was way too cold for November, but she just wanted him to see it. As she struggled with getting her wedding dress off, she noticed some stains and crumbles on the old carpet, and her nose wrinkled when she also noticed some long black hair. It was probably the maid's. Bahrus had told her that they had a woman in the house that took care of all the housework. That had been a good argument to convince her mother and uncle that she should not wait till she had finished her Master programme to get married. She could not wait another two years while her beauty faded, and everybody would start to talk about her as a spinster. Bahrus was more mature and seemed less desperate. She had been in love before, and once she was even talking to a boy on the phone, and even though a lot of boys had been interested, she had never given in to anybody. In the end, they all turned out to be immature boys stalking her desperately. After getting her bachelor's degree, Shiawa had hoped to settle down, but with no engagement ring, she had decided to continue university and hoped she would meet her future husband. It was only a plus she would get an education, too.

Lara sat in her parents´ kitchen drinking tea with her mum and two sisters when she saw the lights being switched on in her house on the other side of the main road in Banaman. The house she had cleaned for nine years…the terrace she had washed for nine years… the trees and bushes she had planted in the garden nine years ago…all her hard work was now being taken over by a new wife just because she could not produce any children. The anger, shame, and all these years' bitterness burnt inside her.

Naturally, her parents, sisters and brother were on her side and had not gone to the wedding.

"Bahrus is just an animal," her mum told her.

"Yes, in the name of Allah he is," Lara said. "I don't understand why I deserve to get married to a man who causes me this much pain.

I was polite when his mum advised me to eat dates and always sleep on my right side to get pregnant. I appreciated they took me to all the best doctors in Hewler and Sulaimania. Even though we had lost hope after three years, I agreed on going with them to Iran and

Turkey," she said and sighed. Her mum and sisters nodded, and Lara continued.

"I even followed the advice of the female sheik in Bestora and slept with a big piece of meat on my stomach for a week, and when it didn't help, we bought a new piece of meat and repeated the procedure. All that money wasted on meat. I even ruined some of our best bed sheets despite sleeping on bin bags."

"Yes, you told us," her sister Roshgar said, but Lara ignored her.

"It was a difficult time, my girl," her mother said. "At least Bahrus told both you and his family to stop all the fuss."

"Yes, I suppose I should be grateful, but since then he hasn't spent a single night in our bedroom." She looked at her mum and sisters, but they all stared into their half empty tea glasses. Sure, they all hated him for always turning his head after every pretty girl in Banaman, trying to impress them with his fancy clothes and car, but it was Allah's will not to give Lara children. What could they do?

"Have I not done everything to make him happy?" Lara caught her sister's look and took a Kleenex and kept it in her hand after wiping her nose.

"Yes, in the name of Allah you have," her sister Ramia answered.

"Have I not made him fried eggs and tea in the morning every day when he was just a Peshmerga, a simple soldier working the two-week shifts?

"Yes, in the name of Allah you have," her sister Roshgar answered.

"Did I not endure the loneliness when he was away for these two weeks? Did I ever complain?"

The sisters exchanged looks. They did remember the whining every fortnight when their sister came back to their house, but it would be unfair to say anything against their older sister when she was in this state of mind.

Lara did not wait for an answer. She had done everything she was asked to do. The only advice she had never followed was to ask Bahrus to change his working schedule, so that he would be home the other two weeks and working the other days, but she doubted this advice from a new English doctor so much that she could even get herself to tell this silly thing to her husband. She and Bahrus had gone to school together, and when they fell in love with each other, both families thought it would be best for them to settle down before a mistake would happen. It was a fine match. Lara was from a good family that descended back to the Prophet Mohammed.

"Eh!" Her father called from the living room where he sat with a bottle of whiskey in front of the television – as always – and shouted orders in the direction of the kitchen.

"What Baba?" Ramia said as she entered the living room.

He didn't look at her. He just said "ice" and knocked on the empty bowl with his glass as a little toast.

"Yes, Baba, I'll bring it now." She rushed back to the kitchen and got the ice out of the freezer. She banged on a big cylinder-shaped piece of ice from an old plastic bucket which had contained Iranian yoghurt and all the noise made Lara quiet for a while.

Ramia went back into the living room with the ice, and Roshgar poured Lara and their mother another glass of cinnamon flavoured tea from the kettle with a big scoopful of sugar.

"Where is your brother?" their mother asked.

"I don't know," said Roshgar.

When Ramia got back from serving the ice, they continued the conversation.

"You're still his first wife, dear Lara. The second wife has to respect you," her mother said.

"Bah!" Lara sighed. "Bahrus has told me that nothing will change since I'll still have the "responsibility" of the house, while the princess is studying. I will end up as her servant this way because I will have to cook and clean for her as well. But I'll never do her laundry, mum, how can I?"

She started to weep and put her head down into her mum's lap.

"Don't cry my girl. Don't cry. It is nothing. We've all been through difficult situations, and you'll overcome this as well. Trust in Allah, and everything will be all right. Sooner or later Kak Bahrus will realise he is making a big mistake tonight."

Lara got up and wiped her eyes with a new Kleenex. She was not ugly and used to be a reasonably pretty girl, but she had gained a lot of weight over the years from eating all kinds of hormones due to the infertility treatments, plus, she tended to reward herself with sweets, chocolate, and her mother's homemade date cakes –whenever things went too sour for her – which they often did. She was only thirty years old, but her hair was strained with grey even though her sisters repeatedly had told her to her to dye it with henna. Her chubby chin and cheeks were hanging on her face and wrinkles had already appeared around her upper lip and right between her eyes that gave her some sort of a malicious look. Her teeth were yellow from drinking too much tea, and nobody blamed Bahrus that much for not having any children with her – at least not now when she looked more like a forty-five-year-old woman. She looked out of the window and stared at her home across the street. A shadow appeared on the terrace. It was undoubtedly Bahrus. He was probably smoking a cigarette. She took out her pink mobile phone that was lying on the plastic kitchen table and dialled his number. She looked at her sisters and mother.

"I will never let him forget that I am his first wife," she said. "Never!"

Bahrus felt his mobile phone vibrating in his pocket. He got it out and saw Lara was calling him. He breathed heavily and let it ring. He was not really in the mood to talk to her now, and the fact that she was calling him right now made him annoyed. He had the right to remarry when his wife was not able to give him any children. She ought to be more patient, really, and understand his situation better. The phone kept vibrating. It was her fifth call now, and he felt a hint of bad consciousness. He knew she would continue to call him the entire night and feel miserable. He picked up.

"Yes?"

"Hello, dear Bahrus."

"Hi Lara, how are you?" He blew cigarette smoke into the air.

"I'm fine, thank you. Peace be upon you. I just wanted to congratulate you with your new wife."

"Thank you very much." His lips turned downwards in surprise.

"How was the party?" Lara continued.

"It was ok," he replied, even though he had spent a fortune on all the extravagance with the decoration, the fireworks and the cameras on the cranes. Shiawa had quietly asked for it, and he just could not say no to all her sweet words that flowed from her mouth. He smiled. The thought of her made him drop his cigarette to the ground to step on it.

"Why did you not ask me about getting a second wife instead of leaving Kurdistan to get an Iraqi marriage certificate?" she asked. "You know that my family would approve of a second wife anyway."

"Oh, please Lara! It is my wedding day." he said.

"I'm sorry, Bahrus."

"Why would I ask you if I knew the answer? I have already heard your uncle in the mosque talking about this several times." Bahrus said. "Besides, I did not want you to wait for hours and hours in a crowded court in Hewler to sign the declaration. On the contrary, I wanted to spare you from announcing to everybody in court that you are not able to conceive."

His words made her quiet.

"Well, it is late," he continued. "Just take your time in your parents' house, and then I'll see you soon."

"Ok" she said, "God be with you."

"Thank you, goodbye."

"Goodbye." she whispered, and then they both hung up.

He went upstairs and opened the door to the bedroom. His beautiful wife sat on the bed in a white night gown and with satisfaction painted on his face, he closed the door – eyes fixed on his bride.

The next morning, Bahrus and Shiawa woke up early to the sound of the mullah calling for prayer from the mosque. Bahrus sent Shiawa an awkward smile.

"What would you like for breakfast?" Shiawa asked.

"Nothing," Bahrus said. He got out of bed and tiptoed on the cold floor to the wardrobe to get his bathrobe.

"Don't you normally eat breakfast?" she asked and sat up in bed.

"Well, sometimes, but we should eat together on our first day of marriage, right?"

"You're right," she said.

"I feel like a new man, dear Shiawa. I want to go to the mosque and do my prayers first."

Without waiting for an answer, he went downstairs to wash his face and brush his teeth. Shiawa heard the door close. The moment he was gone, she shot out of bed, put on a warm shawl she fished out of her suitcase, and ran down the stairs. She peeked into the guest room. Hmm, his mother probably decorated this, she thought to herself. She opened the door to the other living room, wrinkled her nose and thought about some decoration ideas to make it look nicer. She wanted to see the room next to the kitchen, but it was locked – probably the maid's room. Everything looked neat and clean, and she was already satisfied with the woman working in the house. She wondered where she was from: Nepal maybe or Indonesia perhaps. The Indonesians were better. A maid! It was just so luxurious! She knew her mother and uncle never would have approved of the marriage if she should give up her studies to become a housewife, and she sent Bahrus a positive thought for being so clever to import a maid to convince her family that she would not be doing any housework at all. She had gotten this far and even though she never really liked agriculture, it just happened to be the education the government had chosen for her to do, and now she was determined to get her master's, so she would be able to support Bahrus in the green houses.

In the mosque, all the men in Banaman were congratulating Bahrus on his marriage. Bahrus sat next to his friend, Ari, and they did their prayers together. When they were about to leave, Mullah Yusuf came up to congratulate him.

"Congratulations, Kak Bahrus. If Allah wills it, your marriage will be a happy one."

"Thank you, Mullah Yusuf, may peace be upon you."

"Now I will tell you something," Mullah Yusuf said and looked at Bahrus with his big goggle eyes. "Remember, dear Kaka Bahrus, that Allah has been merciful upon you and given you a second wife who can give you a son if Allah (peace be upon Him) wills it. However, it is very important that you do your very best to treat both your wives equally."

Bahrus' smile disappeared. "I am sorry Mullah Yusuf, I know Lara Xan is your niece, but the love between us has died many years ago."

Mullah Yusuf gave him a stern look, "This is not a good sign, Kak Bahrus," he said and pulled his long beard. "Follow my advice, and the angels will write it in the book." Then he turned around nodding at both Bahrus and the men around him.

When the black clad man was out of hearing distance, Bahrus leaned towards Ari and whispered, "How can I love both my wives equally when I am crazy about my new, young, beautiful wife and cannot stand the sight of the other who has only caused me problems?" Ari smiled and said "Well, that is not a problem I am familiar with as I luckily only have one wife."

After a quick shower in the cold bathroom, Shiawa slipped into one of her new velvet nightgowns and went back into the kitchen. She looked in the fridge and got out fig jam, yoghurt, cheese and olives. There was Kurdish bread in a big red plastic tray on top of the fridge, and she stretched on her toes and took two large pieces and gently sprinkled them with water to soften the thin crisp bread. She took two spoonsful of black tea from a jar next to the stove and put it into the kettle with cold water, set the table, and waited patiently for Bahrus to return from the mosque. Finally, she heard his footsteps approaching the house.

"Do you want an egg?" she asked when he had settled into a kitchen chair.

"No, thank you. This is enough," he replied and started to rip off a piece of bread.

She did not want her hair to smell of fried eggs, so she did not insist. Instead, she served the tea and put the sugar bowl next to him since she did not know how sweet he wanted it. She added a spoonful for herself. They ate in silence.

"Did you sleep well?" Bahrus asked after a while.

"Yes, thank you," she said, and fiddled with her bread before putting it into her mouth.

"What do you want to do today?" he continued and started to shovel yoghurt up with his bread and sipped the tea. He realised there was not any sugar in the tea and reached out for the sugar bowl.

"I don't know. It is up to you," she said.

"Do you want to go to Duhok? It'll be our first picnic together. We can stay in a motel for a night and enjoy ourselves," he suggested.

"Sounds good," she replied.

He tasted the tea and frowned. Now it was too sweet. He was not used to adding sugar to his tea himself. Lara normally did that.

"How is the tea?" Shiawa asked sensing his attention to his tea glass.

"It is great," he smiled.

After they finished their breakfast and she had cleaned the kitchen, she went upstairs to pack a little bag with their necessities for the trip to Duhok. Bahrus was waiting outside next to his car with a cigarette in his mouth. He looked at the green Mercedes he had inherited when his father had bought the Land Cruiser. It was old, but he still loved that car. Shiawa got out her sunglasses as soon as she sat in the car and off they went. They went up the mountain to Masif Sallahadin. At the check point the Peshmergas greeted them friendly, and with a wave of a hand let them pass without any problems.

The weather was still sunny and warm during the day. The Mercedes had style, but it was old, and the fan was broken, so they soon rolled down the windows to let some fresh air in. Shiawa felt hot in her new outfit, the same beige, long, fitted jacket with golden white flowers over the beige long skirt she had worn the day they got Mullah Yusuf's blessings before the wedding.

At the next check point in Shaqlawa, they passed a local farmer who had all his blue and red buckets of fresh milk and homemade yoghurt on colourful display.

"Do you want some?" Bahrus said as he turned to Shiawa.

"It will probably turn bad on the long way to Duhok and back," she said.

"You're right," he agreed.

After they passed Shaqlawa, Bahrus pointed out the window towards the magnificent mountains.

"This is the area where I was stationed as a Peshmerga," he said proudly. "The Turkish Kurdish guerrilla fighters shot at Iraqi Kurds, but then it was decided to make a new road exactly as far away, so the bullets could not reach them. Smart, right?" He grinned.

Shiawa looked at him.

"It was also here that the American soldiers once jumped out of their war planes and realised that Kurdistan's mountains were too freezing cold for their desert outfit. Ha! Can you imagine that?" He laughed loudly and shifted in the seat and clapped his leg with one hand.

Herds of sheep and shepherds on donkeys walked around the brown fields. Here and there laundry was hung on homemade fences made of branches or pieces of scrap metal to dry in the sun. The Kurdish elections were in less than a week, and posters had gone up everywhere with different representatives in various Kurdish outfits showing a pointer finger black with ink from voting.

They stopped at a side road restaurant for lunch and sat down outside on the terrace at a table with a greasy plastic tablecloth and old bottles with lemon juice and ketchup. A waiter joined them.

"What do you serve here?" Bahrus asked the waiter.

"Chicken skewers, meat skewers, kebab, and beans," he replied in a monotone voice without even looking at them.

"What do you want to eat?" Bahrus turned to Shiawa.

"I don't know," she said.

"Well, let's have a grill mix then," Bahrus decided.

The view from the terrace overlooked the mountains, and Shiawa got out her camera.

"Can you ask the waiter to take a photo of us?" she asked Bahrus.

"Sure" he said, so when the servant returned with water, and a starter consisting of a tomato-cucumber salad and some olives, Bahrus moved closer to Shiawa, and the waiter took a photo of them. Neither of them smiled into the camera, so they would get an appropriate photo. It would be embarrassing if they were both smiling into the camera.

After lunch, they continued through the mountains to Duhok. From time to time, Bahrus took Shiawa's hand and gave it a little squeeze and smiled to her. When they reached Duhok, they went straight to Mazi Supermarket and bought a walnut Swiss roll decorated with little red cherries, juices, nuts, and other supplies that could sweeten their stay.

The suite in Karwan Motel was brand new.

"It is very nice, but it's too big for us," Shiawa said and went from room to room.

"Everything for you, dear Shiawa." Bahrus smiled at her.

Both showered and changed into fresh clothes, had a cup of tea and then set off for the amusement park – Dream City next to Mazi Supermarket. Shiawa did not want to try anything but preferred just to walk around and admire all the lights and eat her popcorn. It was cold in the evening, so she was wearing a poncho (also a gift from Bahrus), and she loved the feeling of Bahrus' artificial leather jacket on her naked arm. He took her hand, and they walked around like proper newlyweds until they headed back to the motel in the Mercedes.

The day after, they ate breakfast in the little motel kitchen and then packed their stuff and left the motel to explore the dam right outside the city. There was no wind, and the dam was dead still. The surrounding mountains mirrored in the water. The beautiful scenery made them stop and they got out of the car to have their photo taken. Bahrus also took a photo of his car.

They drove past tahini sellers and reached the town of Amedi, where they took a tour around the town on the surreal plateau rising dramatically from the bottom of the valley. There were hardly any cars on the road. Next to a tiny village, two little girls appeared on the roadside selling nuts, and Shiawa bought a few bags just to make them happy. Later, they ate rice and beans in tomato sauce in another dirty restaurant, but at least it was very cheap, and the tea was quite good. The next hour or so, they just admired the views of the mountains.

"You don't need to tell people about our trip." Bahrus suddenly said when they were nearly at home.

"Why not?" Shiawa looked at him in surprise.

Bahrus avoided her look and stared at the road in front of him.

"People will just get jealous and we have to protect ourselves from evil eyes, you know."

"But I like to tell people about my honeymoon," she said and looked out the window.

"Why should I lie about such a wonderful thing?"

"You don't understand my situation," Bahrus said. "Please, just listen to me, and trust that I'm right about this."

"Okay, I will," Shiawa said.

The rest of the trip they drove in silence, apart from the sound of Bahrus continuously munching on a bag of chips.

When they got to Masif Sallahadin, it was late afternoon, and Bahrus suggested that they visit his parents. Shiawa agreed. His mother greeted them in the driveway and invited them in. Shiawa sat down next to Bahrus in the fine living room that was reserved for visitors. Bahrus' sisters brought tea and watermelon and stared at her and she looked down, and she could not eat a thing, frightened that melon juice or a seed might fall on the fine carpet.

"Did you have a nice trip?" Bahrus' sister asked.

"It was ok," he said. Shiawa looked at Bahrus.

"How much did you pay for the motel?" Bahrus' mother asked.

"Fifty dollars," Bahrus said even though it had cost ninety-five dollars per night.

"That is very expensive. Why did not you go to Jihan Hotel? The rooms there are just thirty-five dollars per night, and they're just fine," Bahrus' mum continued.

"Yes, I know mum, but they did not have any vacant rooms," he added. Surprised to hear Bahrus was lying to his mum, Shiawa looked up again, but still found her sister in laws' eyes resting upon her. She just wanted to leave.

When they reached home, they were both tired after the long journey. She did not understand why she could not say the truth about the honeymoon, and she did not understand her husband on this point. Anyway, who said they were supposed to understand each other one hundred percent just because they had been living together for twenty-four hours? She did not expect him to understand everything about her, so why should she be able to understand him? She took a deep breath and felt better.

Bahrus' mother had given them a big plate of dolma to eat when they got home, and after dinner they drank tea and ate the rest of the walnut Swiss roll on the terrace.

"Please excuse me, I'm going to bed," Shiawa said even though it was only ten o' clock.

"Ok, goodnight," he said and glanced at her.

When Bahrus heard Shiawa close the door to their bedroom, he went outside to smoke. He took out his mobile and dialled Lara's number.

"Hi Lara, how are you?" he asked "How are your parents, your brother and sisters?

"Thank you so much for calling," Lara said.

"Why don't you return to the house tomorrow, so you can meet my new wife?" he asked.

"I might have to go to the doctor in Hewler with my mother, but I'll call you if it doesn't get too late," Lara answered.

"Ok, then, sleep well," he said and switched off the phone before she had a chance to say goodbye.

Titles

The next morning, Lara got up early and finally dyed her hair with henna. It took several hours, and she used a dozen of old towels and scarves in the process. Her sister, Roshgar, helped her with removing all unwanted hair on her body, and afterwards gave her a facial mask and a massage. Her sister, Ramia, made Serupe in the kitchen, which was a long process. She cleaned the sheep's stomach on the kitchen tiles near the drain, while running water from the hose rinsed the area. She had already cleaned the sheep's head, which lay grinning in the pot waiting to be cooked. There was an unpleasant smell of death that made Lara sad. Her dad had taken her mum to the doctor. She had high blood pressure and was not feeling well these days.

Only Lara had married in the family. Her brother and her sisters had never married because they could never agree on the quality of a future wife or husband. Only Lara had stood up for herself and demanded that either her parents would never see any grandchildren, or they should let her marry Bahrus. It was a tragedy that they with four children did not have any grandchildren, but her mother never whined about it. She had a strong belief in Allah, and she trusted in her family's destiny. They agreed on the marriage, even though Bahrus was way below their level, but it was not easy to find a good husband.

"Should I go over there now?" Lara asked her sisters.

"No, wait till after lunch. That's better. Else he will just think you are too interested in returning to the house." Ramia said. "And besides, I am making 'head and foot' and will be offended if you are not joining us for lunch after all this hard work," she smiled while she brushed some hair away from her face with the hand that was holding the knife.

"Ok, then I'll wait just because of the poor sheep," Lara sighed and made her sisters laugh. She was fiddling with a Kleenex but now she put it on the table and started to clench her hands, looking out the window, watching her house constantly. She did not speak to anybody.

Shiawa got up and washed the terrace that was dusty after a few days without any cleaning. When she finished, she sat down on a red plastic chair to let her half-wet skirt dry in the sun and admired the clean tiles and enjoyed the fresh air. She had put a scarf around her hair, and the hard work had made her sweat a little. When Bahrus entered the terrace, he raised his eyebrows.

"Don't do this hard work, my love. Lara will probably come home today and do it," he said.

"Lara?" Shiawa asked. "Is she Kurdish? I imagined she would be from Nepal or Indonesia."

"Why would you think such a thing?" Bahrus said and smiled a little.

"Well, most maids in Kurdistan are from these two countries, I've heard," she said.

"I don't like you to call her 'maid', Shiawa."

"Why not?" she said.

"I don't like it. It is disrespectful," he replied.

"What would you like me to call her then?" she asked.

"I think you should just call her Lara Xan," he said.

"An honourable title like Xan? Isn't this a little bit too much?" she asked.

"No, why? After all, we have to be polite to each other since we have to live together."

"But I am your wife. She should call me Xan." Her voice trembled.

"Yes, but Lara is also my wife and frankly speaking, she was in the house before you," Bahrus said.

Shiawa stared at him.

"What do you mean?" she said.

"Lara is my first wife. I got married to her nine years ago."

She looked at him in disbelief.

"Did you not know you are the second wife?" Bahrus said raising his eyebrows. "I already told your uncle. He was here before we got married."

"I don't think he would keep quiet about such a thing." Shiawa said.

"I thought your whole family knew," he said. "I thought you loved me even though I was already married. I was too young to think when I got married the first time."

"But I thought…" The confusion made one of her eyebrows go up. Bahrus sat down on a chair next to her and laid his arm around her.

"Do you know what?" he said. "I really don't love Lara any longer. I haven't touched her in many, many years. Trust me, Shiawa. I only love you, but you must also understand my obligations towards her. You know it is inappropriate to get divorced since I can afford a house for both of you, and she hasn't done anything wrong except that she can't have children. I don't love her, but I do feel responsible for her, and I don't want to make a drama."

Shiawa did not say anything. She just sat there on the red plastic chair and stared into the air. How could she be so naïve? How many had known about this before her? She could not believe she was such a donkey to marry an already married man.

They sat there next to each other without saying anything for a while.

"But why did you not tell me?" Now she looked at him.

"I was embarrassed to tell you directly. I thought your uncle or mum had told you," he said.

"I don't think that I can stay with another wife," Shiawa said still staring into the air. Her entire body shivered from the scary thought of leaving the man she just got married to a few days ago.

She finally turned to him and said: "Does my mother know about this as well?"

"I think so," he said and then she finally broke down and put her head in her hands and started to cry.

"Dear Shiawa, don't be sad. Please, don't be sad." Bahrus touched her hair, but she turned her head away. "Shiawa, my love, Lara doesn't mean anything to me. She is just very practical to have in the house. Think of it; you get to take a degree, and she must do all the housework. When you come home, you can relax, you can study, we can go out, and whatever you want. You are younger than her, more beautiful, cleverer. Please don't be angry with me. I did not want to keep it a secret, and I discussed this with your uncle. I thought you would still love me even though I once made the mistake of marrying the wrong woman. Please don't punish me for that." He lit a cigarette.

Shiawa got up. "I want to be alone," she said and left him on the terrace and went upstairs. She lay down on the bed, pulled the blanket over her head and cried.

It was nearly noon when she woke up. Her head was hurting, and her body felt heavy. She sat up but could not move out of the bed. She let her chin touch her chest and her legs just dangled from the bed. She knew she had to make a decision now that would affect the rest of her life. She was in love with Bahrus, and she knew he loved her as well. She knew she would have very little chance to remarry and have children if she decided to divorce him – and she really wanted a family. For a moment, a few blissful days, she had felt happy. She had felt she belonged. She longed for her mother to discuss this with, but her mother had known about this all along, so what kind of advice could she possibly give her? How could her mother possibly think that she would be happy to be someone's second wife because his first wife could not conceive? She heard Bahrus' steps on the stairs, and it was time for her to make up her mind. He opened the door and sat down on the bed.

"Can't you ask her to stay with her parents?" she asked.

"But your family said it was a condition that you should not do any housework, so you could focus on your studies," he answered.

"You're right," she said, "but she can just come and do the housework and sleep in her family's house."

"But Shiawa this would be very inappropriate," Bahrus said.

"I know, but I just can't imagine myself having a life with you when another bitter woman who is also your wife is living in the same house," she could hear her voice tremble.

"Shiawa, she means absolutely nothing to me. She sleeps downstairs in her own room, and we sleep up here in our room."

"But I don't want her to be here at all."

"I am promising you, when you finish your Master's, I'll ask her to move, but right now I cannot give up my promise to your family."

She looked up. The thought of her family made her wipe her eyes. She had never thought about it in this way. Even though she was angry with both her uncle and mother for not letting her know the truth about Bahrus' first wife, she could not really blame him because he had told them, and her family had still thought he was good enough for her. She had to respect them, and she had to respect Allah's will, too.

"Do you promise that she'll leave when I finish my Master's?"

"If this is what you want," he answered.

"And are you sure you don't love her?"

"Yes, Shiawa, and when you see her, you will be certain about this," Bahrus said and laid his arm around her. Her body relaxed under his touch.

"I don't want to lose you now that I've finally married you." She cried into his shoulder.

"And I don't want to lose you either," he said. "Don't worry, everything will be just fine."

They hugged each other for a long time, and Bahrus invited her to Valentine Restaurant on the Masif Sallahadin highway where they had rice and beans in tomato sauce.

The Encounter

"Am I pretty?" Shiawa asked Bahrus and looked down at her Kurdish dress. It was one of her new dresses.

"Yes, in the name of Allah you're pretty."

They both sat in the living room on the couch and waited for Lara to show up when they heard the keys in the door.

"Why does she not knock?" Shiawa asked. "Why is she intruding like this when we are at home?"

As soon as the door opened, Bahrus got up and went towards her.

"Salaam Aleikum," Lara said when she walked across the threshold.

"Aleikum Salaam," they both echoed. Shiawa stood up in respect for her and shook her hand lightly.

Bahrus introduced them to each other. "This is Lara Xan, my first wife," he said, "and Lara, this is my new wife, Shiawa Xan."

Silence fell while Lara looked Shiawa up and down. Shiawa did not know where to look, but the look of Lara in her black abbaiya, her long shiny black hair and her evil look gave her goose bumps. Right then she regretted her decision to stay with Bahrus, but she told herself she just had to endure two years with this woman, and she promised herself that she would overcome the future problems she knew she now had to face. She felt her knees shaking.

"Welcome to Banaman," Lara finally said.

"Thank you."

Lara went into the kitchen right away.

"Oh, it is so dirty here. How can people live in such a mess?" she shouted.

She banged the pots, plates and cutlery around the kitchen, and Shiawa looked at Bahrus with her eyes wide open. With a gesture of his hand he let her know not to worry about it. Shiawa went upstairs and found her books and decided to study. She opened a book about how to keep sheep, turned to page one, and started to read the introduction:

"Sheep (Ovis aries) are quadrupedal, ruminant unclemals typically kept as livestock. Like all ruminants, sheep are members of the order Artiodactyla, the even-toed ungulates."

She did not understand a word, skipped the rest of the introduction, and flipped through the book until her eyes fell on a drawing that was describing the biology of a ram, but she could not focus. She constantly heard Lara moving around in the kitchen. She turned the pages here and there and read the text under an illustration of a sheep's tail which was about the importance of shearing the area around the tail to avoid the fly maggots from eating the sheep's butt. She did not know what to use this information for. The climate in Kurdistan was rather dry, and as far as she knew, scorpions and snakes were far more dangerous than flies. She was recalling how her professors had explained that if a sheep accidently got stung by a scorpion on its leg, you would have to cut up the leg and add red clay directly into the wound, so that the clay could suck up the poison. There was nothing in the book about that. She had to remember to ask her uncle about it. She slammed the book shut and grabbed her drawing book instead and started to sketch the anatomy of the ram. She labelled the different body parts with the Latin names but had to refer to the book several times even though her professor had set it as homework to remember the Latin names by heart. She had rehearsed it several times, but she felt blank now. If this woman downstairs would just be quiet! Shiawa heard a car coming up the driveway and looked out of the window. It was a crimson coloured Opel Vectra, full of people. The boot of the car was not closed, and she could see an old woman and a little child with a juice box in his hand getting out once the car was still. The old woman stretched her body and adjusted her headscarf over her braided white hair. Shiawa remembered them very well from the wedding. She glanced at herself in the mirror and quickly tucked in her hair under her head scarf and brushed invisible things off her clothes. She ran downstairs, but before she reached the hall, Lara had opened the door and welcomed the guests.

"Welcome. In the name of Allah, welcome, welcome. Please, come in and sit down." Everybody took off their shoes before entering. Lara nodded politely at the men who were the first to enter. Then she kissed the women many times and gave each child a kiss. When the old lady from the trunk came close to her, Lara bent down, took her hand, kissed it, and said, "Dear Baji Xan, welcome." She wiped her eyes hoping nobody noticed, but Baji padded her on the arm and said: "Don't cry. Don't cry, my girl. You are much older than her. You have more experience. This is life. Only Allah knows what is good for us, and you have to accept your destiny."

Baji looked at Shiawa who was standing by the stairs with her hands folded in front of her. "Welcome," Shiawa said and stretched out her hand. The old woman gave her a limp hand, and then she entered the living room that was reserved for guests only and sat down heavily with the rest of the family, who seemed to feel at home. Lara switched on the television and found an Arab-speaking Sponge Bob for the kids.

"Peace be upon you and welcome everyone!" Bahrus said when he entered the living room.

They all got up from the sofas they had just sat sunk into. "Thank you very much. We hope you're well," they all answered.

When Shiawa wanted to follow after Bahrus, Lara stepped in front of her and blocked her way and made her the last person to enter.

"Welcome," Shiawa repeated inside the living room, but her voice was so little that nobody seemed to hear her. There was nowhere to sit, so both Lara and Shiawa stood up for a while before Shiawa went into the kitchen to fetch the big box of Ferrero Rocher she and Bahrus had bought in Mazi Supermarket in Duhok. She served it for everybody, who thanked her and unfolded the golden paper and ate the chocolate. She offered Lara one, but she just looked at her and exclaimed "Is this what you give people to celebrate this marriage?" Lara passed her with her chin up and sat down on the floor close to Baji.

Shiawa did not say anything. She placed the chocolates on the coffee table and sat down on the floor next to Bahrus.

"How is it going with the greenhouses, Kak Bahrus?" Baji's husband asked.

"Not too bad, thank you, but it is very difficult to manage". He tried to sound as natural as possible to hide the very fact that things were going great in the greenhouses, and that he had made a fortune this summer. November was the end of the season, and around New

Year he would clean out the greenhouses, cultivate, and get ready to sow in February.

"And how are your parents, Kak Bahrus?" Baji asked.

"They're very well, Al hamdu li lah," he replied.

"And how is your mother and uncle, Shiawa Xan?" Baji asked, finally addressing the bride.

Shiawa bent her head, smiled and said: "Thank you, they are very well."

She did not know how to continue the conversation. Her mother and uncle used to speak whenever they had guests, and usually she would just sit with the kids or girls her own age and whisper and giggle. Baji's husband asked Bahrus some other questions about the work in the greenhouses and Shiawa got up and went into the kitchen to make tea for the visitors. When she left the living room, Lara also got up and followed her into the kitchen.

Baji interrupted the men's conversation; "Kak Bahrus, don't forget to treat your wives exactly the same way, or there will be a lot of unhappiness under your roof as if an owl had landed on it."

"Inshallah, I'll do my best," he said.

"Don't pay too much attention to your new wife in the beginning. She will just get used to it and demand more and more from you. It is better to be a little strict from start and then loosen the grip later." At this point, Baji pointed a knowing finger at him.

"You're right, Baji Xan," Bahrus smiled, and then he turned to her husband to continue their conversation about a new technique that had been introduced by the German – Kurdish Agricultural Association about putting up a net to get a cucumber plant to grow bigger and in this way to get more cucumbers. Bahrus had participated in a workshop where he had learnt everything about how to install the nets instead of just having the plants growing on the ground and in this way take up too much room in the green house.

"I already bought the nets in the bazaar," Bahrus said.

"Good for you!" Baji's husband exclaimed, and that was the end of the cucumber conversation.

In the kitchen, Shiawa put the kettle on after having added the black tea.

"Did you use the tap water!?" Lara exclaimed. Her entire body had frozen.

"Yes, why not? The water boils, so it will be clean," Shiawa said.

"No, when we have visitors, I always use the good water from the bottles. Only the best is good enough for the visitors of this house," she said.

"No problem, I'll change it," Shiawa said and emptied the cold water with all the tea leaves into the sink. She found the bottled water, added the tea and put it back onto the gas burner.

Lara Xan went into the pantry, and when she returned, she lifted the lid of the tea pot. "Did you not add any cinnamon sticks?" she asked. "Kak Bahrus loves that, so I always make it with cinnamon, and he says he loves my tea."

"He has never complained about the tea I've served either," Shiawa said.

"Of course not, you just got married." And from the back of the cupboard she took out a plastic bag with whole cinnamon and added it to the tea water without consulting Shiawa any further.

"Where do I find a tray?" Shiawa asked.

"On top of the refrigerator, under the breadbasket," Lara said.

"Where are the tea glasses you use for guests?" Shiawa asked.

Lara sighed and after a short pause, she pointed to her left. "They are in the cupboard over there."

Shiawa got out the crystal tea glasses and arranged them on the tray with a teaspoon and a spoonful of sugar in each glass. She found the little tea strainer, and then they waited for the tea to be nice and strong. Lara put the homemade cakes on a tray. There was baklava, date cakes, and round decorated cakes filled with walnuts, sugar and cinnamon. Shiawa did not really know what to do, but Lara was very busy. She was cleaning the kitchen sink of all the tea leaves, washing her hands, putting some glasses away, swapping the teaspoons Shiawa had found with some other teaspoons, adding a tiny bit of extra sugar to the tea glasses. She took the lid of the teapot and poured a little bit into the sink. She wrinkled her nose, and Shiawa saw it.

"I think it needs to boil a little bit longer," Shiawa said.

"Well, we can't really let the visitors wait the whole day for a cup of tea, can we?" And then she poured the tea into the glasses, went off with the cakes, and left the tray for Shiawa to bring in.

Shiawa's hands were shaking when she brought in the tea. She kneeled on the thick carpet and put the tray on the little coffee table and gave each guest a tea glass.

"Oh, you've already taught Shiawa to serve tea, Lara Xan. That is very good," Baji said. Shiawa's face turned red and she thought to herself that people in Hewler also serve tea for their guests.

"These date cakes are really nice. Did you make them yourself, Shiawa Xan?" Baji's daughter-in-law asked and looked at the little date cake.

"No, I did not," Shiawa said feeling Lara's eyes resting on her. She did not know who had made them, and she did not like to ask, and she did not have to.

"My sister Roshgar made these." Lara said. "It is so nice to have a sister who can help and support you at all times."

"Al hamdu li lah, Lara Xan. My sister also makes me cakes, dolma and bread and brings me fruit and sweets and everything. It is really really nice." Baji's daughter-in-law answered.

"How are your sisters?" Lara asked.

"Al hamdu li lah, they are fine," she said and turned towards Shiawa.

"How many sisters and brothers do you have Shiawa Xan?" she asked.

"I am an only child," Shiawa replied.

"Oh, really?"

"Yes, my father was a martyr."

"Aww, poor her." Baji's daughter-in-law turned towards Lara. "How unfortunate she is. I know that she lost her father, but I did not know she did not have any brothers and sisters. Poor her. That is very difficult." And then they both looked at her with pity.

"How is your mother, Shiawa Xan?" Baji asked.

"Al hamdu li lah, she is fine, thank you very much Baji Xan." Shiawa said.

The conversation went on for a while about other insignificant elements of false politeness that were being exchanged in the living room. Then Baji looked at her husband who nodded.

"We really should get going," Baji's husband announced.

"No why, it's so early?" Shiawa, Lara, and Bahrus more or less said at the same time.

Nevertheless, they all stood up, thanked each other and left under just as much noise as when they came.

Bahrus went to the greenhouses to check how things were going, and Shiawa tidied up the living room, and went into the kitchen. Lara had gone to her room, and all the dirty dishes stood all over the kitchen table, and she decided to do the dishes even though it really was not her job. She opened a new packet of rubber gloves to protect her hands from the dish washing liquid and spent half an hour in the kitchen. She had nearly finished when Bahrus entered.

"Dear Shiawa, don't make yourself tired doing the dishes," he said. He came up to her and put an arm around her, dipped his head into her hair and smelled her peach and honey shampoo. She could not do anything else than just stand there with her rubber glove hands on the dirty dishes, but she enjoyed his attention and leaned back just a little. Right at that moment, Lara came into the kitchen, opened her mouth without a word and then spun around and hurried outside where they could hear her turn on the tap and start to wash the terrace even though Shiawa had already cleaned it. Bahrus and Shiawa giggled and smiled to each other.

"What can we do?" Bahrus said and kissed her on her cheek. "We are newlyweds."

The three of them ate dinner in silence. Tea, yoghurt, bread, cheese and olives. After dinner, Bahrus pushed his plate to the middle of the table, brushed the crumbs off his hands and went outside to smoke a cigarette. Lara went straight to the bathroom to take a shower, and again Shiawa was left with the dirty dishes. There weren't that many, and she understood that it was hard for Lara to suddenly share the house with a new woman, so she decided just to do it. Tomorrow, she had classes, so she could relax then. She heard Bahrus enter the house again and turn on the television to watch the news. She finished the dishes and put on the kettle to make a cup of tea and arranged a tray with mugs and a big bowl of sunflower seeds with a plate of grapes. When she came into the living room, Lara and Bahrus were sitting on the same couch watching the news. She felt a pain in her stomach at the sight of them. It looked so natural for them to sit together even though they were far apart, but it did not prevent her from feeling that she was intruding. She left the tray on the coffee table in front of them, so they could serve themselves and sat down in an armchair with a cup of tea. Lara poured the tea for Bahrus, added sugar, and scooped up a bowl of nuts and kernels for him as a movie started. Shiawa tried not to look too much into their direction but stared at the television.

It was getting late, the movie had finished and now there was a program about the increasing amount of scorpions in Halabja, and Shiawa started to yawn and sent Bahrus a look from time to time, but he seemed to be rather interested in the program, and she did not catch his eye. When it was nearly eleven o´clock, she couldn't endure her tiredness any longer and got up.

"Good night," she said.

Lara continued cracking sunflower seeds and only stared at her, but Bahrus looked at her and then his watch in surprise.

"Oh, yes, it is late. I think I also want to go to bed now."

Shiawa smiled, and when he got up and followed her to hunt her up the stairs, she could not avoid letting a little laughter out. Lara took another handful of sunflower seeds in the living room, but apart from that she did not move her heavy body.

The next morning, Shiawa got up at seven. Bahrus was in the mosque and she had not even heard him leave, so she ate breakfast alone – even though she wished she had the time to wait for him. The dirty tea glasses and the bowl from last night were still on the kitchen table. She quickly washed everything, put on her makeup and got her bag, and then got down to the main road where she caught the university bus.

Before the first class started, she kissed all her friends and had to tell them all about her honeymoon and her first few days of her marriage. Her closest friend, Sahar, had participated in the wedding and had heard about the first wife. She was furious on Shiawa's behalf and pulled her friend away from the others. Despite her anger, she tried to whisper:

"Shiawa, why do you accept these circumstances? In the name of Allah, how dare he treat women like that? Even our Prime Minister is against polygamy! Bahrus is a very charming man, and I consider him my brother, but he should just divorce his first wife and not take advantage of both of you." Some of the other students looked at them as Sahar's whisper got louder.

"I know about it, Sahar. All the men in this country want to die in wars, so we can't be too picky." She tried to make fun of the situation.

"Honestly, Shiawa, I know you don't mean that. He did not tell you about this, did he?" Sahar asked.

"You don't understand…" was the only thing she managed to reply. Then the bell rang, and it was time for class, and she did not have to answer or explain herself.

Shiawa looked worried after listening to Sahar. Maybe Sahar was right, but she had already decided to stay.

The lesson was about natural and organic pesticides and fertilizers, and Shiawa half listened to the lecture while the other half was thinking of Bahrus and Sahar's words. After the lecture, Sahar went home because she was too tired to stay on campus before the start of the afternoon lecture, but Shiawa went to buy lunch in the cafeteria and then waited for her second class in the library. It was a long day.

When the university bus finally dropped her off in Banaman, it was nearly half past five. She walked up the long driveway. When she got closer to the house, she could hear Bahrus and Lara's voices from the terrace.

"It is getting very late, Kak Bahrus. Where is your wife? Do you just let her run around by herself the whole day? Do you call this a wife?" Lara insisted on getting an answer.

"She is studying. Don't be unreasonable." Bahrus defended Shiawa.

"But why did you marry her then if she is not even here? This doesn't make sense to me at all," said Lara.

Shiawa kicked a few rocks lying and even made a fake cough and pretended she had not heard anything. They looked at her.

"Salam Aleikum," she said.

"Aleikum Salam," they replied.

Bahrus looked relieved, but Lara simply turned around and left them on the terrace.

"How was your day?" Bahrus asked and smiled.

"Not bad," she said and sat down in a plastic chair. He put an arm around her and kissed her hair while Sahar's words vanished from her mind, and she turned into a girl in love.

"Do you want to come and have a look at the greenhouses?" he asked, and she was happy to get away with him and not be near Lara.

Bahrus had three greenhouses where he mainly grew aubergine, tomatoes, green pepper, and squash. He told her about his plans to grow cucumber next season using the new technique he had learnt, and she kept nodding as he spoke. He was so clever.

"What type of fertilizers are you going to use?" she asked, remembering some bits from the day's lecture.

"Oh, I haven't really thought it through," he said.

"Maybe you should prepare the soil now and then the soil will be perfect to sow in February," she said.

"Oh, you are so clever even though you haven't even graduated yet." He poked her arm.

"Maybe I can use this experiment in my thesis?" She was thinking aloud.

"Yes, why not? It sounds perfect. Then I will have an extra worker and even an educated one to keep an eye on the progress, and I won't have to pay her a single dinar."

Shiawa smiled at him. She loved him when he was this silly. But an idea had been planted in her, and she was just as interested in growing cucumbers as Bahrus was. They decided to go for a walk up to the little castle where a princess once used to rule the surrounding area. There were many steps up, and when they reached the top of the hill, the sun was setting. The pollution from the increasing number of cars in Hewler made a beautiful sunset, and they just stood there admiring it.

Noises from the village reached them. Down the hill, Baji and a few other women and children, who had been out walking, ran in all kinds of directions because they had woken up a wild dog who was now hunting them. It snapped Baji in her leg, and she screamed loudly and frightened the dog even more which just made it bite again. The children were fast and ran up the hill, but the women ran towards a nearby house and banged on the porch to get in. Fortunately, the man of the house had watched the scene and as he opened the door to let the screaming women inside, he snatched his revolver from his belt and shot the dog who was still hunting Baji. The dog immediately fell to the ground, and all the kids ran back to examine the dead animal. Shiawa and Bahrus went down the hill. Their house was right at the bottom of the hill where Princess Khanzad had once built her little castle. They went to see Baji. Her leg did not look good.

"I'm okay, I'm okay, don't make a fuss," she said, but she moaned when the other women helped her back to her house.

When they got home, Lara was not there, but from the terrace they could see her walk across the main road and find her way to her parents' house.

"What do you want for dinner?" Shiawa said. She was starving.

"Oh, I am not really hungry. Lara Xan made dolma for lunch, and I ate too much. Maybe there are leftovers you can heat." He padded his belly and smiled, satisfied.

Shiawa went into the kitchen and found a plate of left-over dolma that she heated while she wondered how Lara and Bahrus had eaten lunch together. Had they been sitting across each other, next to each other, or had Lara been serving Bahrus and waited to eat till after he had finished? She knew it did not mean anything, but it did not change the uncomfortable feeling she felt in her throat. The dolma was with small pieces of meat and tasted good, but she thought it was a luxury to serve this dish on an ordinary day. After taking just a single bite, she threw the rest on her plate in the bin.

Rain and Mud

A little more than a month passed, and it started to rain more often, and the temperature dropped to around fifteen degrees. The roads in Banaman got muddy and in many places the big puddles made it impossible for people to leave their houses by car. The women pulled up their colourful Kurdish velvet night gowns and tried to make it to the neighbour's house without getting too mud stained. Shiawa still got on her bus in the morning and attended her classes, while Bahrus and Lara stayed at home together. Bahrus had very little work to do in the green houses, so he spent a lot of time in front of the television watching the news while Lara served him breakfast, lunch and afternoon tea and fruit in the living room, and both of them also watched a new Brazilian series in the early afternoon before Shiawa returned.

Shiawa felt she had put herself into a position where she had to do the dishes. Nobody had told her to, but the dishes from the night before were always waiting for her in the morning, and it was stressful for her to clean the kitchen before leaving in the morning. In the evening, she did the dishes after they had eaten dinner, but since she left the living room as the first one to go to bed, she couldn't do the dishes that late. She did not dare to touch the snacks on the coffee table in front of Lara. They still received many guests at the weekend or visited Bahrus' parents or her mother and uncle, but because of the rain, most people considered it inappropriate to turn up with muddy sandals in a house that might have been flooded with rainwater.

After doing the dishes, she went to the bathroom to brush her teeth as the last thing this morning. First, she was puzzled not to find her toothbrush in the mug, but then she realised it had landed on the bathroom floor. She took a final glance at herself in the mirror, and then she went upstairs to her room where she put a warm scarf around her head and grabbed her books before she ran downstairs. Outside, her boots had been put away from the corner near the door and laid in the rain. She ran upstairs to find another pair and ran all the way down to the main road, but it was too late to catch the university bus. She was late.

She only waited for about ten minutes before a taxi stopped, but by then she was soaked because of the heavy rain. There were already two women in the taxi, an old woman and a younger woman who was probably her daughter, and they were willing to share the fare to Hewler. They exchanged a few formalities, but most of the time Shiawa looked out on the rain. Her feet were wet and cold, and the old woman in the front seat was constantly burping, which made her sick to her stomach.

Lara woke up late and decided to visit her family. There were leftovers for lunch, so she did not have to cook today. She reached her parents' house and went inside the kitchen where her sisters were busy peeling pear quinces for jam. Baji was also there eating sunflower seeds and discussing all the events in Banaman. They had already talked about Lara and Shiawa, and now Baji was in the middle of showing them where she got bitten by the dog.

"Welcome," they all greeted Lara.

"Thank you," Lara said.

Ramia got up and put the kettle on before Lara had even sat down.

"How are you doing, Lara Xan?" Baji asked.

"Thank you, Baji Xan," Lara said. She hesitated for a second but then continued. "You know I'm really against gossip, and I really don't like to say anything bad about Shiawa, but… she never lifts a finger to help with the housework. I do the cooking, I do the cleaning, and I serve my husband. She doesn't do anything."

"Oh, that's very inappropriate," Baji said.

"What he sees in her, I find very hard to understand. She is not even that pretty."

Everybody nodded apart from Baji who seemed to be thinking.

"Her eyes are too big, her hair is not very shiny, and she hardly wears any makeup. Did you not notice?" Lara said.

Baji wrinkled her nose and Ramia nodded, but everybody else kept eating the sunflower seeds, waiting for other news Lara brought.

"She just comes home late in the afternoon, and then she eats my food and spends the evening in the living room either reading or drawing male animals. Can you believe it?"

Baji stopped eating the sunflower seeds and looked at her.

"And every single evening she tries to seduce Kak Bahrus by going to bed really, really early, but thanks to Allah, he usually stays with me," she said.

"What do you mean? Does he sleep in your room now?" her sister Ramia asked.

"No, not exactly my sister, but I mean he stays with me in the living room for a while, and then he goes upstairs to their new bedroom later."

"But really this is not right," Lara's sister said as she was trying hard to cut the quince. "I heard mother was speaking to uncle Yusuf about it, and he said, that when a man takes a second wife, he should make sure he treats them the exact same way. Tell Kak Bahrus this. He really should sleep in your room every other night."

"But he will never accept that, he hasn't touched me in years!" Lara said. "He has just been fooling around with other girls on his motorcycle, inviting them out to fancy restaurants to smoke water pipe. How can I suddenly make him change? It is even harder now."

"Just make him realize what a good wife you are despite the fact that you cannot get pregnant," Baji said.

Lara stopped talking for a while and bit her cheek. "Yes, it might be a good idea," she finally said and started to drink her tea.

Their mother entered the kitchen.

"How are you doing my girl?" she asked Lara and sat down.

"I am fine, mother. Thank you."

Ramia left her seat and got her mum a glass of tea.

"I heard you were talking about my brother. What were you talking about?" She looked at all of them one by one.

"Mom, isn't it true that Uncle Yusuf says it is very important to treat wives equally?" Ramia asked.

"Yes, this is common knowledge. It has always been like this," she said. "It is just because only very few men take another wife these days that we hardly talk about it any longer."

"It is true," Baji added. "Most men in Banaman are not rich and cannot afford another wife even though many of them probably dream about a new younger model to spoil instead of listening to us." She chuckled, but the other women did not react.

"Unfortunately, Lara Xan, most people think Kak Bahrus is in his good right to remarry and keep two wives because you cannot conceive, and after all, he is the richest man in the village," Baji said.

"But mom, please talk to Uncle Yusuf and ask him to speak to Kak Bahrus about this. It is very inappropriate what he is doing," Lara said.

The conversation was interrupted by Lara's brother who entered the kitchen and looked inside the fridge. He found a cold chicken leg, which he started to eat.

"Do you know Kak Bahrus is treating Lara Xan in a very bad way?" Ramia said.

"Hmm?" he said and kept eating.

"Why don't you go and speak to Bahrus now? Lara Xan is here, and he is at home with Shiawa. Go and tell him he should come to his senses and treat his wives equally," his mum said.

"Ok, I will speak to him, but I am just on my way to the gym, so I'll do it later." He was only in his thirties but already half bald, with too big a belly.

"When are you getting married?" Baji asked him. "Think about your poor parents."

"Oh, I have been wanting a wife for the past fifteen years, but whenever I announce I have found the love of my life, a good girl from a respectable family, all my sisters find all kinds of flaws."

"Oh, I'm sorry to hear that." Baji did not expect his honesty.

"Well, they have promised they will find me a tall and fair wife from a good family. Isn't it true, sisters?" He looked at them.

"Yes, brother, but first, we have to deal with Bahrus' second wife." Ramia said.

"You see, Baji Xan. This is why I'm not married," their brother said. "I believe I still have a chance, but I don't want my future wife to be disgusted by me, and that's why I have started to work out."

"That is very good, my boy," Baji said.

He was about to leave the kitchen but stopped by Lara and pretended he was about to give her a brotherly kiss on the cheek on his way out. "Besides, I do not want to miss the chance to watch the women from the parking lot when they leave the gym," he whispered into her ear.

"You are an animal," she whispered back. Fortunately, Baji did not hear very well.

Friday

Mullah Yusuf liked to share his knowledge and wisdom with as many people as possible, and apart from his Quran study groups and his assistance in Jalil Xayat's mosque, he also preached in Banaman mosque on Fridays. As the old mullah entered Banaman mosque, he noticed a pickup full of dirty construction builders driving into the small dirt parking lot. He stopped, and with his stern look, watched them as they were laughing and joking while washing their feet, hands, and face before entering the mosque. He sighed and went inside. When all the men had settled, he took the microphone in his hand and started to talk.

"Life is like a door – you enter, and you leave. Under all circumstances, it is important to maintain the highest hygiene. Once upon a time, a lot of young men were working on Fridays as construction builders even though the holy Quran clearly states that everybody should keep Friday holy and not work. These men had taken a bath in the morning, but after hours of hard and dusty work, it was time for prayer, and they all rushed to the mosque to pray after splashing a few drops of water in their face and on their hands and feet. What do you think about this?" Mullah Yusuf recognised some of the men from the pickup and maintained eye contact with one man until the man looked down."

"Clearly, this is not good enough." Mullah Yusuf coughed." Taking a bath on Fridays is mandatory for every male Muslim who has attained the age of puberty. If you go to the mosque in the first hour after your bath, it is as if you have sacrificed two lambs, but if you go in the fifth hour after a bath, it is as if you have just sacrificed an egg."

Some of the men shifted their weight from one leg to the other. Mullah Yusif raised his voice.

"I have lived in Holland for eleven and a half years with my wife and children who are all studying at the university there." He raised a hand into the air and pointed towards the ceiling. "I single-handedly carried out several terrorist acts against Holland. First, I was sentenced to a couple of years in prison for making death threats against Dutch officials, and this year I got kicked out of the country. Despite facing all this adversity, I have always been clean in my mind as well as my body." Mullah Yusuf sighed into the microphone and decided to move on with his personal story.

"Upon my arrival in Kurdistan, I immediately got the job in Jalil Xiyat's mosque, and do you think I would have gotten a job in the biggest and most beautiful mosque in Kurdistan if I hadn't been a good mullah – a clean man, eh? It is built by one of the richest families in Hewler who have donated the mosque to the inhabitants of Hewler. It has been under construction for more than ten years, but yes, this is also clearly visible. It is breath-taking, and all the employees feel pride in working there, and so do I; a clean and honest man who remembers to come clean to the mosque." He thought he had made his point clear now and moved on.

Despite the weather, Lara's mother had invited her brother Mullah Yusuf for lunch after the Friday prayer in Banaman mosque. Her daughters had made kofta, the heavy round balls filled with minced meat, sultanas, almonds, and parsley in a sauce made from curried chickpeas. They ate lunch together in the kitchen.

"It was a good thing that you talked about hygiene in today's ceremony," Lara's dad said after lunch when they sat in the living room where Ramia served tea and freshly made date cakes. Lara sat down-right next to her uncle and started to fiddle with a loose thread in the carpet.

"How is it going with your husband and the new wife?" Mullah Yusuf asked Lara.

"Very well, thank you, Uncle Yusuf," she said. "He is very fond of her, and they spend a lot of time together," she lied because she was the one who spent most of the time with Bahrus - just not during the nights.

"Well, that is a common mistake many men make when they take a second wife, but just be patient and see if this doesn't change after a while." Then he took the tea glass to his lips and took a date cake.

"But really dear brother," Lara's mother interrupted, "isn't it too much to ask one to be even more patient when this person has already faced so much adversity in life? Her husband hasn't slept a single night with her after he got married to his second wife!"

Mullah Yusuf stopped chewing and carefully brushed a few crumbs off his beard. Then he looked up and gazed at his sister. "It is clearly a violation of the Islamic rules to treat your wives differently, and I will make sure that Kak Bahrus does not misuse this rule, and I will personally go to see him later today and have a word with him." Then he took one more date cake from the crystal plate, asked for a pillow, and fell asleep on the sofa.

Mullah Yusuf paid Bahrus a visit the same evening after having his nap in his sister's house. Bahrus and Shiawa had had a lovely day together without being bothered by the presence of Lara. Shiawa opened the door and led the mullah into the living room where Bahrus was watching television.

"Kaka Bahrus, I've come to talk to you about something important," Mullah Yusuf said when he was comfortably seated in the armchair.

"Oh, no, what have I done wrong this time, Mullah Yusuf?" Bahrus smiled.

Shiawa came in with coffee, but as she wasn't invited to sit down, she left the door open and went upstairs to study. She did not close the door and held her breath in order to hear what the old mullah wanted to talk to Bahrus about.

"You know I've lived in Holland for nearly twelve years, right? "Mullah Yusuf did not wait for an answer. "And I've gained a lot of experience in matters between husband and wife."

"Oh, I see, did Lara ask you to come and see me?" Bahrus broke him off.

"Ehem, no, but people talk, and you know it's my duty to talk to you," Mullah Yusuf said.

"Of course," Bahrus said.

"According to Islam, it is all right to have two wives, but it is crucial to treat them the exact same way. My niece tells me that you always spend most of your time with your second wife, and this creates an unbalance in your house which is not healthy for either you or your wives." Mullah Yusuf looked at Bahrus and waited for a response, but Bahrus just looked at the flowery pattern on the carpet.

"Do you pray?" Mullah Yusuf asked.

"Yes, five times a day," Bahrus answered.

"Good, good. Do you fast during the Ramadan?"

"Yes, of course," Bahrus said.

"Very good, very good. Then it should not be difficult for you to honour Allah by treating your wives equally."

"With all respect, Mullah Yusuf, my second wife is away from home most of the day because she is doing her Master's in Hewler, so the entire day I am with my first wife. I eat breakfast and lunch with my first wife, and then we all eat dinner together and watch TV together. In fact, I wish I could spend more time alone with my new wife," Bahrus defended himself.

"Hmm, but I am not only thinking about the hours you're awake. I am also thinking about the time when you switch off the lights in your house. And it would be best if you could, ehem… share your nights between your wives, so they don't feel one is better than the other."

"Ok thank you for your advice, Mullah Yusuf. I'll try to make them both happier," Bahrus said.

"Very well, I think it's time for me to leave then." Mullah Yusuf felt he had done his duty, stood up, shook Bahrus' hand and left with a few polite goodbyes. Outside he looked towards the sky and mumbled a short sura from the Quran and with steady steps he walked towards the road.

Bahrus went upstairs. He stopped in the doorway and admired his wife, who was absorbed in a book about growing cucumbers in greenhouses. He looked at her tiny wrists and hands holding the thick book. She looked up from her book and smiled at him, and he came in and sat on the bed.

"I have something to tell you," she said with her tiny voice. "I am pregnant."

"Really?" He said, "but…, but we just got married."

"Yes, I know, but I took a test, and I went to the doctor, and it is true. You are going to be a father."

"Oh, that is, that is wonderful!" And then he went to her side of the bed and hugged her a little too hard. Shiawa was so proud of herself. Just one month after their wedding she was pregnant. She had already told her mother who had shared her happiness, and immediately started to plan all the baby items she would sew on her sewing machine. Shiawa was not sure about whether she would be able to finish her MA now, but she would not let that disturb her happiness. She was Bahrus' wife. She was going to give him children, and Lara was not.

"You know what?" Bahrus said, "I think we should open an account for our little baby, and every dinar we earn on the cucumbers should go to our little monkey."

"That is a wonderful idea. Then we'll both be working extra hard on making that project a success," Shiawa added.

"Yes, I hope it is a good investment," Bahrus said.

"Me too," Shiawa added.

"But don't tell anybody about it," Bahrus suddenly said.

"About what?" Shiawa asked.

"About everything," Bahrus said. He looked at his wife's face and said; "I don't want to attract evil spirits."

"But I've already told my mother that I'm pregnant, and Sahar also knows because she went with me to the doctor."

"Just keep quiet about it here in Banaman then," he finished.

Shiawa nodded and grabbed her book again, and Bahrus got up and went downstairs.

Saturday passed as usual with visitors and visiting Bahrus' family in Masif. The following Sunday when Shiawa was back at college, Bahrus opened the account for the baby in her name.

"One thousand dollars!" she exclaimed when he gave her the bank statement upon her return.

"I just wanted you to feel that I really mean what I promised," he said.

"Thank you.'" They hugged, but then they heard Lara rumble around the kitchen, and Shiawa put the bank statement straight into her bag. She knew Lara went through her stuff when she was away, and she did not want her to know about this. Lara was from a rich family, and she did not need the money, but she understood that Bahrus' kind gestures had to be hidden.

Mourning

New Year's passed and January turned cold, and everybody constantly spoke about the Russian snowstorms. None of the houses in Banaman were insulated, and it was freezing cold indoors. In the bathroom, big ice crystals formed on the tiled walls because it was constantly moist and cold, and in the windowsill in the living room, lay big chunks of ice from the windows' constant production of condense water. They used little electric heaters to heat the house with, but because of the wet weather there were more frequent power cuts, and then they had to use the kerosene heaters. This evening, the only light came from the kitchen, and it was snowing. It was rarely this cold in Banaman, but this year was an exception. Even the pipes froze in many houses and left them without water. The pipes had been frozen for a week, and Shiawa had not been able to bathe and her hair was flat and greasy.

"Oh Bahrus, please take off your muddy shoes outside," Shiawa snapped when Bahrus finally came inside after trying to melt the ice in the pipes on the roof with several kettles full of hot water. He looked at her but did not bother to answer. She was extremely tired and nauseous because of the pregnancy, especially in the evening. Bahrus noticed the change.

The next day around lunchtime, Bahrus and Lara went to visit Lara's family. Bahrus was making an extremely bored face to Shiawa with his eyes looking upwards when he left, indicating he was now going to spend a few horrible hours with his in-laws. So far, he had not followed Mullah Yusuf's advice about spending nights with Lara, but today he had agreed on accepting the lunch invitation from his in-laws as he sometimes did have some scary thoughts about how he one day would be punished for not caring about his first wife.

"So, Shiawa seems a little pale these days," Lara said as they were walking towards her parent's house.

"Hmm?" Bahrus said.

"Shiawa is vomiting quite often," Lara said.

"I think it's normal," Bahrus said.

"Why is it normal?" Lara asked.

"It's normal because she is pregnant," Bahrus said and straightened his back which made her shrink. When they reached Lara's family's house, he was several steps ahead of her.

They rolled out the plastic tablecloth on the floor as there were too many too sit around the table. Lara's mother had made brown and sticky pomegranate rice and little meatballs, and there was lots of salad, herbs and bread.

"Have you heard that Baji has gone crazy?" Lara's dad asked.

"No. Really? Was it because she was bitten by the dog?" Bahrus asked.

"Yes. I guess it is that illness you get from dogs. Her husband told me she suddenly started to vomit, got a fever, has no appetite and has a bad headache. She also has a lot of spit around her mouth and her eyes are constantly full of tears."

"Allah is great." Bahrus said.

"Yes, poor lady," Lara's mother said. "Later, she found it really difficult to swallow any kind of food or liquids, and now she is afraid of watching a glass of water and suddenly starts to run around in the house."

"That's terrible. What can we do?" Bahrus said.

Shiawa did not like that Bahrus had left, but she understood why he had to. When they had left, she went into the garden and banged on the ice in the water tank and tried to scoop water into a small casserole and then into a big old vinegar bottle she could bring into the house. She stood on a big brick, but it was still difficult to reach the water and she had to stretch her entire body. Inside the house she put a pot of water on the kerosene heater, added some Tide washing powder, and then her underwear since she obviously could not use the washing machine without electricity. She stirred her underwear around in the pot, threw out the dirty water and fetched another bottle of water to rinse the laundry with. It was a long tiresome process, and the moment she had finished hanging up the clothes outside in the cold sunshine, she lay down on the floor to rest and fell asleep wrapped in a woollen blanket in front of the kerosene heater in the kitchen.

When Shiawa woke up later, she felt dizzy from the kerosene. She got up and opened a window to let the cold air enter the kitchen and put on a shawl before she went outside to see if her underwear was dry. It wasn't dry but just frozen. She sighed from regret. Now it would be too late to dry it before Lara came back with Bahrus. She should have known that the temperature was below zero despite the sunshine. She wanted to lift the dry cloth stand, but when she did, it collapsed on the terrace and most of the clothes fell onto the ground and even into the garden. Now it was all dirty again, and she started to cry as she picked up the frozen bras and knickers. Back inside, she put two pieces of chocolate in her mouth and wiped her nose and put the underwear back into the pot, put on her shawl and went into the garden again to collect water as she had done several hours earlier.

January turned into late February. It was still cold and wet, but it was time to make the cucumber plants in the green houses where there was no longer any risk of frost. After dinner, one of Lara's sisters came to visit and Bahrus and Shiawa were working together adding good soil to little pots and sowing the cucumber seeds and enjoying the quiet green houses. Now they were just making little plants. They would plant them out later. Suddenly, they heard an enormous explosion, and they looked out through the door of the green house. On the main road to Masif, two cars had crashed, and an old pickup had exploded. The other car was a Land Cruiser and a man was lying on top of the car as the air bag had not worked. There was a big hole in the windscreen where he had flown out. Three trees in between the opposite lanes were in flames. Bahrus could see men and boys in Banaman getting into motion. The little boys were running excitedly to get close to the accident to see more. The younger men were running to see if they could be of any assistance and maybe turn into heroes afterwards, and the elderly men wanted to see what was happening and come with their advice if needed. Bahrus took off his gardening gloves and placed them on a barrel while still looking at the road. He squeezed his eyes together to see better. A creeping feeling of fear ran from his feet to his stomach. He walked out of the green house without saying anything to Shiawa who stayed back as it would be very inappropriate for her to go and stare directly at an accident. Once Bahrus got closer to the cars, he started to run. People turned the motionless driver around and put him on the ground, and now Bahrus recognised the bullet holes in the Land Cruiser and his father laying there on the wet mud with a lot of blood oozing out of his head.

"Baba, Baba, Baba", Bahrus fell on his knees next to his father.

People lay down and listened to his heart and took his pulse, but he was dead. The police arrived and guided the curious cars away from the accident. The men tried to calm down Bahrus and told him to take it easy, but he pushed them away. Then he started to cry sitting on the ground next to his Baba. He cried for the first time in a very long time. Just five minutes ago he was happy. Happy with Shiawa and happy about soon becoming a father after all these hopeless years with Lara. Happy about his success with the green houses. Why was he not allowed to let it continue? Why was he not allowed to show his new-born baby to his father and share the proud feeling with him? An ambulance came and took the unknown burnt pickup driver with them while the people of Banaman took the body of Bahrus' father to his son's house. Bahrus walked behind the people who carried his father's dead body across the road and up to his house. From time to time, he started to cry and let his fingers run over his eyebrows as if to ease the pain.

Shiawa had followed the incident from the greenhouse, and when she saw the men returning to their house she walked back as fast as she could without running. The men had put the body in the middle of the living room and placed a pillow under the still bleeding head, and a sheet covering the entire body. Bahrus went to the bathroom and, while weeping, washed his feet, hands and face. When he came into the living room, he took the Quran from the windowsill and sat down beside his father and started to read a sura, but before finishing he started to cry again.

"Dear Baba, dear Baba." He leaned over the body and cried uncontrollably.

The rest of the men prayed together. Afterwards, they sat in silence and mourned together with Bahrus. The sound of a washing machine made one of the men look up and glance towards the door.

It was Lara who had started to do laundry. She had already started one wash and was sorting out clothes while talking to her sister Ramia.

"Now, I will be so busy with guests, so it's better to get it done now before the house gets too full of people," she said.

"Yes, that's right," her sister said.

Shiawa went into the kitchen where women from Banaman had already taken over the kitchen and were preparing tea. Then she went into the living room and sat down on the floor close to the door. She could not cry because she had only known Bahrus' father for a few months, and she had hardly ever spoken to him since she was too shy to say anything to him. But the sight of her mourning husband made her sad and the atmosphere of death was creeping around the floors, melting into the chilly air in the living room. They had not turned on the heat.

As soon as they knew, all the inhabitants in Banaman went to Bahrus' house to pay their respect to Bahrus' father. Bahrus' family also came down from Masif. When they saw Bahrus sitting next to the man of their family they all broke down and started to cry. Bahrus' oldest sister started to hit herself on the head and pulled her hair while she was screaming and tossing her body around.

"Stop it! It is inappropriate to behave so madly," Bahrus' brother pulled her arm hard, and she calmed herself down.

The closest family sat around the body. They were rocking back and forth while Bahrus tried to read verses from the Quran even though he started to cry sometimes. From time to time, one of Bahrus' sisters threw her body over their father and wailed. His mother sat motionless on a chair, staring into the air without seeing.

They waited for Mullah Yusuf to arrive. It was already dark and too late to go to the graveyard, so they had to wait till the morning to bury the body. At one stage, the women were asked to leave the room so they could wash the body. Shiawa went to the other living room with the other women. A lot of people were already gathered there, and it was getting crowded. It was getting late, and people were encouraging each other to go home and sleep, but nobody liked to be the first one to leave. After all, they were all mourning the loss. After midnight, Lara and her sister got out mattresses and warm blankets so that family members and friends could lie down and relax. Shiawa heard Lara argue with Bahrus' mother.

"Mother of Bahrus, let the memorial take place in our house tomorrow. Then you don't have to worry about anything." Lara said.

"But Lara, he is my husband. I like to have it in our own house." Bahrus' mother protested.

"Everybody is already here and Bahrus' father is going to be buried here tomorrow. Mullah Yusuf is already on his way."

"I really don't like it." Bahrus' mother said and sighed. "But very well. Tomorrow it can be here, but on day two and three the mourning should take place in our house."

Mullah Yusuf arrived at one in the morning and took over the reading of the Quran. Most people from Banaman, who weren't related to Bahrus, decided to leave, apart from Lara's sister. Mullah Yusuf kept reading the entire night with the family. Shiawa went upstairs but only slept a few hours.

As soon as it dawned, the men went to the mosque with the body and buried it on the little hill opposite Khanzad castle. It was a very old graveyard where little rocks from hundreds of years ago signalled that they had survived wind and weather to tell the tales of the dead warriors, blacksmiths, and farmers buried underneath. Apart from Bahrus' mother and sisters, who had gone with the men to see their father leaving this world for good, the women stayed at home, but a female mullah came to the house to chant and pray with them. The living room was already crowded with women. The mullah's assistant carried a drum and with the sound of her drum and reciting of the Quran, soon everybody was rocking back and forth, chanting, head banging and praying together. It was a loud mass mourning act. Suddenly, a woman started to pray, and the rest started to pray together with her. Then silence.

Still early morning, Lara's brother brought two sheep that were slaughtered in the back yard by some of the more experienced men in the village. He also brought several boxes of frozen chicken, ten sacks of rice, water, vegetables, fruit and sweet baklava. He had rented a pickup for the purpose, and Lara looked very pleased with his help. She was planning on serving the visitors well even though it was expensive, and a group of people were already busy in the kitchen peeling onions and cutting up green peppers for a Tishrib dish, while another group were making salad, a third group cleaning the chicken, and a final group arranging trays of tea glasses and water that were circulating the house. People were buzzing around doing this and that.

"Shiawa, can you please give me the tray," Lara said.

"Of course," Shiawa said. She noticed that the other women paid attention to the fact that they were talking together. At one point, Shiawa sneaked away and briefly lay down on the bed in her room upstairs before she – with great effort – pulled herself out of bed and went into the living room again.

As she entered the cold room, all the women turned around and looked at her. Bahrus' mother and sisters had returned, and the men were now sitting in the mosque. Shiawa sat with the women for a while. In between prayers, drums, and outburst of cries, the women were gossiping about everything.

"What is wrong with your arm since you have a bandage on it?" an old abbaiya-clad woman asked another woman in a similar outfit. They blended well with the whole flock of black crows.

"Oh, I burnt myself on the gas oven. You know these ovens don't work and suddenly it exploded while I was standing right next to it. Al hamdu li lah, it is only this arm that got burnt."

Everyone was quiet for a noticeable time.

"Where is my bag?" a woman suddenly asked herself. After looking around the mess of naked feet and black folds of cloth, she finally found it under her abbaiya and got out her mobile phone and called someone.

Right before lunch time, Shiawa went back into the kitchen. The Tishrib, the rich tomato soup, had boiled for hours and the meat was now falling off the big bones. She squatted down next to the big trays and started to scoop soup into little bowls from huge pots someone had brought and set up in the kitchen for the occasion.

There were hundreds of guests, and Shiawa filled tray after tray with bowls of hot soup. Soon her legs felt numb from resting her behind on them, and blisters were appearing since the big wooden spoon was carving into her skin on her hands.

"Oh, Shiawa is working," someone told one of the other abbaiya clad women and smiled to her.

"We have heard that you never lift a finger, but now we can see that you are just as helpful as anybody else," a young woman revealed.

Shiawa just smiled back at them.

When it was time for lunch, they rolled out long disposable plastic tablecloths all over the floor and arranged the plates, cutlery and glasses on them. The women were sitting back to back eating. Some of the neighbours had brought a huge pot of Biryani. Everyone discussed the food.

"Well done, it's very nice."

"Yes, very nice, but the Tishrib is a bit salty, right?

"Did you see they slaughtered two goats?"

Some of the women quickly snatched the roasted chicken with their greasy fingers and did not even care about wiping their mouth. It made Shiawa sick to watch. She had a small portion of food and then went into the bathroom to wash her hands and face. She looked at herself in the mirror and saw a tired face looking back at her. Her pregnancy still made her nauseous and tired.

Bahrus let his beard grow and turned quiet in his mourning. Most days, Lara and Shiawa just brought him food and drinks and in general avoided him since he could not focus on a conversation.

After forty days, people visited Bahrus for the final memorial session. It was bound to happen that he overheard a conversation in the corridor from his place in an armchair in the living room.

"Is Allah sending a message to Bahrus and telling him to behave?"

"Yes, it is obvious isn't it? He hasn't exactly been an angel."

That his sins could be linked to his father's death was a thought that tormented Bahrus. Did people genuinely believe it was more than a coincidence that Allah had chosen his father to die right in front his house? Had he not been a good man? Despite his flirtatious nature, he had always been faithful to his wives, but maybe he should have listened to Mullah Yusuf's advice about treating them more equally.

After the memorial service, when everyone had gone home, Bahrus took a mattress and a blanket from the attic and went to sleep in Lara's room. Shiawa had already gone to bed, but Lara was in the kitchen doing the last dishes for a change and nearly fell over Bahrus when she entered her room. After she had gone into bed, she reached out for him and gently stroked his back, but he did not react.

Bahrus continued to sleep every other night in Lara's room. He did not do anything else than sleep, but it was still a hard defeat for Shiawa and a sweet little victory for Lara. Every night that Bahrus slept in Lara's room, Shiawa cried herself to sleep, telling herself that this was not right. This was not a life. This was not worthy for her. But repeatedly, she tried to be sensible and told herself that it was just a period her husband should get over. He would get over it soon. Everybody did. She just had to finish her master's degree, be patient, endure the pain, and then everything would be just fine.

Bahrus could not do anything else than to watch television, eat and sleep. He often went to the mosque where he either prayed or just sat quietly on the carpet with the Quran in his lap. People tried to tell him that it was Allah's will and that he had much to live for. Shiawa took over the management of the green houses. Spring had finally arrived, and it was crucial not to postpone anything related to the little cucumber plants that had to be planted out, and she also had to build the trellis. Lara's father came over one night and tried to distract his son-in-law with a bottle of whiskey and a game of cards. It worked and soon Bahrus was talking and drinking, drinking and talking, and seemed to be livening up for the first time in a very long time. A few hours later, he was getting quite drunk.

"Shiawa! Lara! Bring some food, please," Bahrus yelled and started to laugh. They were starting a new game.

It was ten o' clock in the evening, and Shiawa was getting ready for bed since she had an exam about fruit trees the following morning, and she decided not to react to his rude shouting. She had not learnt anything in her agriculture classes and Uncle Ahmed had to take her to his nursery and explain everything to her from scratch. She had always placed herself behind Bahrus in class where she had been too busy looking at his neck and movements. She had just sat in the classroom pretending she was looking at the white board, when in fact she was staring at Bahrus, longing dreamily to touch him accidently. Once Bahrus caught her gaze before she got a chance to look down, and from that day he invited her out and treated her like a princess, and slowly won her over till the day he suddenly sat in their living room and simply asked her mother and uncle for permission to marry her. She regretted her silly behaviour now.

Lara was already feeling ownership of Bahrus just because he slept every other night in her room, and since she would be sleeping alone this night, she thought it should be Shiawa who should serve their husband, so she also decided not to do anything. Therefore, nobody came into the living room.

"You have two wives but none of them respect you enough to cook you a simple meal when you're hungry," Lara's father said. "Then I prefer one wife and a lot of obedient daughters who make my life pleasant."

Hearing his father-in-law chuckle annoyed Bahrus. He got up and went to Lara's room where he opened the door with such force that she jumped when she saw him. "Cook me a meal!" Bahrus shouted and banged his hand into the door. Lara went into the kitchen without a response and took some eggs out of the fridge and a pan from the cupboard.

Lara's father stopped laughing in the living room when he heard how Bahrus was yelling at his daughter. Shiawa heard the violent movement downstairs and went out of her room and listened from the top of the stairs. On his way back to the living room, Bahrus saw Shiawa standing paralysed on the stairs.

"What are you looking at?" he yelled. "Get down and cook me a meal like my first wife!"

"I have an exam tomorrow, and I need to get some sleep," she said and turned her back to him and started to walk back into the bedroom.

"Don't turn your back on me," Bahrus shouted, and in a second, he got up the stairs and grabbed her by the arm. "Bahrus!" Shiawa exclaimed and tried to get out of his grip. "Just listen to me," Bahrus said and shook her. "Let go of me. It hurts, Bahrus," she said and pulled her arm back with such force that she lost her balance. He tried to catch her with the other arm, but she tumbled and fell down the stairs. Shiawa moaned and wrapped her arms around herself and could not breathe properly. Lara's father got up from the couch in the living room and saw Bahrus on top of the stairs and Shiawa on the ground. "What have you done?" he asked Bahrus. In an awkward manner, he tried to tend to Shiawa, and then called Lara to come and help. Lara went out of the kitchen and looked at Shiawa on the floor, her father, and Bahrus on the stairs. Shiawa kept wrapping her arms around herself and started to cry.

"You don't deserve two wives," Lara's father said. "You don't even deserve my daughter. Mullah Yusuf is right when he says you should treat your wives the same way, but he doesn't mean you should treat them equally bad. Let these women sleep and get some sleep yourself." And with these words, he left the unfinished game of cards and went out of the door shaking his head.

Bahrus had been standing motionless, but now he sat down on the stairs. He put his head in his hands.

"What have I done? What have I done?" He shook his head. "I am sorry Shiawa. I am sorry Lara. I am so sorry. Please forgive me. I am so sorry."

Finally, he got up and went down the stairs where he kneeled beside Shiawa. He put his arm around her. Shiawa had stopped crying, but she still breathed heavily and tried to sit up. She did not look at Bahrus, and kept her head turned away from him. Lara and Bahrus helped her to get up the stairs and back to the bedroom. She did not say goodnight to any of them and just closed the door.

Shiawa did not sleep well that night. She had a nightmare about how Lara had thrown her sandals far away from the house, and when she went outside to get them, Lara locked the door so she could not enter the house again. Bahrus opened the door, smiling, took her hand and led her upstairs, but suddenly pushed her down the stairs, and when she was lying there on the floor, she looked at her stomach and saw a little baby arm come out of the skin holding a little cucumber in its tiny white hand. Then she screamed and woke up. It was still night, and the night was dark. Only Hewler shone like Las Vegas with all its lights. She could see the airport and an early flight landing in the distance.

She had never been on a plane, but right now she wished she could just get on that plane and go far, far away. She knew Bahrus was mourning, but it did not give him the right to treat her like this. She had not done anything wrong that deserved this. She touched her stomach kindly. It was getting bigger. She was now four months pregnant, and it was getting obvious that she was expecting. She was afraid that the fall had damaged the baby, and she turned around and tried to fall asleep again. This time she did not dream.

The next morning, Shiawa felt a strong pain in her stomach and decided to stay at home despite her exam. She knew something was wrong, and she could hardly walk because of the pain. Clearly, she could not walk down the stairs, so she did not eat any breakfast. She did not want to be with Lara or Bahrus and decided just to lie in bed and draw animals the whole day. Bahrus was still snoring in the living room, but she could hear Lara in the kitchen getting breakfast ready. Around lunch time, somebody knocked on the door. Shiawa looked up from her drawing. "Yes," she said, and the door opened, and Lara stepped inside with a tray of food. Neither of them said anything, and Lara just left the tray at the side of the bed and went out of the room again. Shiawa was hungry and started to eat. After the first mouthful, she started to weep and she continued to cry feeling scared that the food might be poisonous, and that she did not have any other opportunity than to eat it. She heard Bahrus went to the bathroom, and shortly after she heard his steps on the stairs. He knocked lightly on the door and opened it.

"How are you feeling?" he said and sat down on the bed.

"I am ok," she answered.

"Weren't you supposed to take an exam today?" he asked.

"It hurts, and I can't walk properly," she said.

"I am so sorry about the way I behaved last night," he said. "I promise you that this will never happen again. Trust me. I am sad that my father passed away. Everybody blames me because of the way I've treated Lara the past many years. It was not just because she could not conceive. She turned fat and ugly within no time after we got married, and the only thing she cared about was to buy new gold bracelets, the colour of our curtains, and the crystal glasses she wanted to serve the tea in. I don't know what to do any longer. You are pregnant, and how can you continue your studies if nobody is at home to take care of the baby?"

"I don't like to continue my studies if it means I have to leave my baby with Lara. Is that what you mean?" she said.

"Who else should look after the baby when both your family and my family live in different towns?" he asked.

"There is absolutely no way that I can give up my baby to somebody who hates me the way Lara Xan does. I'll take the baby with me to Hewler when I have classes," she said. "Some of my friends sometimes leave the babies in the women's prayer room during classes. I can do that, or I can take the baby to my mother, and then I can go home during the breaks. Anything else than Lara Xan stealing my baby. Our baby."

"No, it is not a good idea Shiawa," Bahrus said.

"Bahrus, I think I'll go and stay with my mother again. It is so stressful for me to live in this house," Shiawa said.

"No, Shiawa. It will not solve anything. Please be patient. It would be very inappropriate if you leave, and Lara Xan will just feel she has won the game. You know I love you, and that I don't want to hurt you." He put his arm around her and tried to hug her, but she pushed him away.

"You did hurt me last night," she said.

"I know, but it will never happen again."

"How do I know?"

"Because I love you, Shiawa. And you know what? I've decided to give you one of the green houses. You can have the third one where we grow cucumbers, so that you can track everything and collect information and use the data in your thesis. You can use my men to help you, but all the income is for you and the baby. I will tell my brother to sell everything you grow in his shop."

Shiawa looked up. For the first time in her life, she possessed something valuable that could possibly make her rich.

"Thank you," she said.

Bahrus stopped going to the mosque. He did not like to be reminded of his bad behaviour towards Lara, and now he did not care much about anything but watching TV and playing cards. After Shiawa's accident down the stairs, he did not drink quite as much, and if Lara and Shiawa obeyed him straight away, he did not get angry.

After a few days, Shiawa felt fine again. She now had the full responsibility of the cucumbers. Some of the workers knew what to do in the other two greenhouses, so there was not much to do for Bahrus.

The little cucumber plants were now ready to be planted out, and she managed to get the nets up in nice fine rows. Her mum and uncle visited her for the Kurdish New Year, Nawroz. She, Bahrus, and Lara stayed at home and did not participate in the celebrations because Bahrus' father had recently passed away. The village was empty and quiet apart from some wild dogs and some elderly people, who had had their quota of picnics in their lives and did not bother to sit in a traffic jam for several hours around the picnic resort Hanara.

Her uncle and mother looked at her work in the green house.

"Very organized," Uncle Ahmed said.

"Yes, look at these perfect little cucumber plants," her mother added. Shiawa was beaming with pride.

"How is your health?" Her mum asked her when they came back to the house.

"I'm fine, mother," Shiawa said.

Her mother took out a plastic bag from her bag and gave her a lot of things she had already made for the baby; a little blanket, some socks and a little hat. Shiawa sighed dreamingly and gave her mother a big hug. Lara and Bahrus were polite towards her family, but she clearly sensed that they did not really have any interest in them. Bahrus was yawning because he had gone to bed too late the previous night, and Lara started to vacuum the hallway, so they had to close the door to the living room to be able to hear what each other said. Lara kept banging the vacuum cleaner into the door panels, and the sound interrupted their conversation several times. Shiawa apologised, but her mother and uncle sent each other sceptical looks in a moment they thought Shiawa didn't notice. After all, they had both known about Bahrus' first wife, and could not complain about it now. Shiawa had already told her mum and uncle that Bahrus had given her one of the greenhouses, and her uncle was bold enough to ask Bahrus to come to Hewler the next day.

"If it is not too much work for you, would you mind coming to Hewler and organize the paperwork for Shiawa regarding the greenhouse?" Uncle Ahmed said.

For a moment, Bahrus looked a bit confused as if he had no idea about what Uncle Ahmed was talking about.

"It is just good to have things done the right way, and one of my neighbours has a friend who is a lawyer and can probably give us a reasonable price for going through all the bureaucratic procedures in the ministries.

"I think Shiawa feels that whatever I own, she also owns since we are married, so I don't know whether it is necessary, Shiawa?" He looked at her, but she just looked at the carpet and did not say that she preferred the paperwork done. She was embarrassed to say it out loud, but she really wanted it, and she knew there was no other way to get it than pushing him into doing it. Uncle Ahmed saved her and said to Bahrus: "With all respect Kak Bahrus, you have two wives, and whatever Shiawa and you own, Lara Xan also owns, and it might not be in our family's interest." Shiawa could not hold back a smile. Now there was no return for Bahrus.

"It is not a problem, and if you like, I'll soon come to Hewler to get it done," he said a little too sourly.

"Fine," said Uncle Ahmed. "I'll have the papers ready to sign. Let's say, the day after tomorrow?"

"Inshallah, I'll be there. Thank you very much for your help Uncle Ahmed," Bahrus said, and then Uncle Ahmed and Shiawa's mum started to get ready to leave.

When they left, Shiawa went upstairs into her room and started noting down information about the progress in the green house. According to her calculations, her cucumbers should be ready to harvest at the beginning of May. The seeds had germinated around the first of March, and then it would take about sixty-eight days to grow to a reasonable size. Of course, it would depend on the weather conditions and how much water she would have, so these calculations were simple guesswork.

She had decided to grow a typically short cucumber to maintain the good taste. She had read that in order to make the plant produce cucumbers for as long a time as possible, she would have to pick the cucumbers early. Nothing was as horrible as a giant bitter cucumber. Anyway, she got out her calculator from the drawer – ninety smaller cucumbers throughout the season from each plant and multiplied with the about one thousand plants, she had would add up to a total of ninety thousand cucumbers. Ninety thousand cucumbers! She giggled and kept tapping on the calculator. One small cucumber would weigh around one hundred grams, and if she multiplied this with ninety thousand cucumbers, she suddenly had nine tons of cucumbers in one cucumber season. The kilo price in her brother-in-law's shop was one thousand dinars, so this meant that her harvest would be worth nine million dinars. "Wow!" she said out loud. The number nearly blew her mind. Nine million dinars was the same as seven thousand and two hundred dollars, and if she could grow herbs in between the rows, she would most likely be able to earn twice as much. In the second season, she would probably have difficulties with enough water, so she expected a smaller outcome during these months, but since she would still be able to harvest from May till October, she would be able to earn a lot. She would have to pay the two workers a few hundred dollars per month, but the rest of the money would be hers and hers alone. She already started to think about the things she would buy, and she pictured her baby wearing the best clothes every day. She threw herself back on the bed and smiled to the ceiling.

As the German-Kurdish Agricultural Association had told Bahrus, the purpose of the trellis was to lift the cucumber plants off the ground to increase the number of cucumbers and to decrease the risk of rotten plants and diseases. Also, it was a more effective way to use the limited space in the greenhouse. Shiawa instructed the workers in building the trellises. She had seen this in a book in the university library, and now she was looking at her drawings to tell what the workers had to do. First, they found some lumber around the village. It only took the workers a few hours to build the frames, and since they used old building materials from around the big garbage drops in Banaman, it did not cost them a single dinar. After the builders had made the frames, they put on the net which Bahrus had already bought and it was supposed to be very good for the cucumber vine to grab hold of and climb. This part was slightly more demanding, as the net constantly got tangled. They spent the whole day building the trellises and decided to put them in place the following day.

The next day, the workers dug big holes inside the greenhouse and put the trellises in place. They packed down the soil with their dirty shoes and adjusted the trellises along the rows of the cucumber plants so they could grow up the nets from both sides. Shiawa and the workers were tremendously proud of the result.

"Well done!" She praised the middle-aged men warmly. They smiled at her because it was all new for them, and even though she was a woman and told them what to do, they still liked her because she was always kind towards them.

Haram

April arrived and the cucumber plants were now one month old and had started to grow up the nets. It was all very exciting for Shiawa. One day, some of her male classmates – who were on their way to a picnic in Shaqlawa – stopped by in Banaman to see her work in the greenhouse. Bahrus and Shiawa took them to the greenhouse where they asked questions and took a close look at the installation of the trellises. Shiawa invited them politely home for a cup of tea, and when they entered the hall, Bahrus asked the visitors whether they preferred tea or coffee.

"Oh, don't worry, we'll drink whatever you drink," they all replied.

"No, please let me know what you want. It is not a problem at all," Bahrus insisted.

"Ok then I'll have a cup of coffee," one of them said. The three others preferred tea.

"What do you want, Shiawa?" Bahrus asked.

"Tea," she said. Bahrus acted as if he normally was the one who would care about his wife and visitor's well-being when he confidently went into the kitchen where he asked Lara to make two coffees and four teas. She looked a little confused at him when he requested it, but he just clapped the doorframe as he placed his order.

Shiawa was sitting on the couch when Lara entered with the hot drinks on a tray.

"Welcome," she said and nodded politely to the young men. She started to serve the men who thanked her, but she did not give Shiawa a cup of tea.

"Did you not want a cup of tea?" One of her classmates asked her.

"No, it is all right," she refused.

"Please, take mine," he insisted, but she kept saying no, and finally he drank his own tea. Shiawa was just watching the others enjoying their hot drinks.

Lara went into the kitchen and came back with a plate of date cakes and a huge bowl of fresh fruit and some plates and little fruit knives. Shiawa avoided looking at Lara because she was afraid that her ugly presence would suffocate her. There were only five plates and five knives, and Shiawa understood that Lara was trying to send her another message. Shiawa did not eat or drink with her classmates even though they were all good friends and considered each other brothers and sisters. She was angry to be treated like this, but in a way, she was happy that her classmates were watching the misery she was experiencing. At least, she was not suffering alone.

When the visitors left, Lara went to her parents′ house and Bahrus went to visit his mother.

Lara sat down on a plastic chair in the kitchen with her sisters.

"This girl is unbelievable. Can you imagine what she did today? She invited four young men into our house, and she just sat down in the living room, while I had to make tea and coffee for them and serve them cake and fruit."

"No!" her mother said. "Is it really true?" Lara nodded with a face showing misbelief.

"But where is Kak Bahrus?" her sister, Roshgar, asked.

"He went to visit his mother," Lara said.

"But it is forbidden for a married woman to invite other men into the house when her husband is not at home!" her sister, Ramia, said.

"Yes, I know it is Haram," Lara replied, "but this girl doesn't care about any of our rules. She just does what she wants without caring about anybody else."

"Did you tell Kak Bahrus?" Ramia asked.

"No, I don't want to be the one who is running to him gossiping about his second wife. He will just think that I am jealous, and that I am trying to create problems," Lara said.

"You're right, Lara. That would not be a nice thing to do," her mother said.

"Last month she spent a whole weekend with the workers in the greenhouse, so it is not the first time I experienced this." Lara seemed to be truly upset.

"Why?" questioned her mother.

"Bahrus gave it to her," Lara answered.

"But what is she going to do with it?" Roshgar asked. "How can she work there alone with all the workers? It is really inappropriate."

"She is growing cucumbers," Lara said.

"Cucumbers?" They all said it at the same time.

"Yes, she is drawing sketches of the plants, and writing down a lot of information. I don't know what."

"Oh," her mother said as the only one. "But why?"

"I don't know." Lara replied. "Honestly, this girl is so strange." They all nodded.

One day after class, Shiawa went to visit her mother. Uncle Ahmed was working in his nursery and would not be back till late, but he had left her the papers regarding the greenhouse. Bahrus had not even told her that he had gone to see her uncle, and that he had signed the papers. She opened the plastic folder carefully and had a look at the papers with all the stamps and signatures from different departments and ministries. Now the green house and the five hundred square meter land it stood on was legally hers.

"Are you happy?" her mother asked and looked at her.

"Yes, thank you," she said and hugged her. Then she gently put the paper back into the plastic folder and asked her mum to keep it in a safe place.

"How are you?" her mother asked, and Shiawa was about to tell her how horrible the atmosphere was in the house back home in Banaman, but she did not want to make her mother upset if she told her about what had happened. She wanted to be loyal to her husband.

"I am okay," she said. "I am getting fat, as you can you see." She touched her belly and they both laughed. She had agreed to go to the bazaar with her friend, Sahar, that day. They had arranged to meet at the water fountain below the citadel at two when the shops in the bazaar would open after the midday break. From her mother's house, she took a taxi and got off near the bazaar. Sahar was late as always and there was no sight of her anywhere, so she sat down on a bench opposite the bazaar. The new tall wall around the bazaar matched the beautiful old citadel. It was Hewler's pride, and with good reason. It had been under reconstruction for five years, but it was difficult to see much improvement. The municipality had destroyed a lot of buildings in the middle of the city centre and had kicked out all the poor people from the humble clay-built houses inside the citadel. This was the price of modernity and urban planning.

A man and an elder woman came up to her and interrupted her thoughts. They did not look Kurdish.

"Hello madam, I am an Indian tourist, and this is my mother." He spoke with a heavy Indian accent. "Yesterday, she lost her bag on this bench, and in her bag, she kept her passport and six hundred dollars, which she was supposed to buy a ticket for back to India. Would you be kind and donate some money?" He didn't show any expressions.

"Oh, I'm sure somebody found the bag and brought it to the police station." She knew that if she stood up right now and left without her bag, someone would come running after her with it. People watched each other constantly, and somebody would surely notice the forgotten bag from somewhere.

"But good luck finding the bag!" She ended the conversation and avoided the question of money. The couple left, and at the same time, she saw Sahar getting out of a taxi. She got out from the left side of the taxi, and nearly got run over by a passing car, so she quickly ran across the street. When she came up to Shiawa, she was a little out of breath.

"Sorry, I am late," she said with a smile and kissed Shiawa's cheeks.

"Are you out of your mind? You could lose your virginity when you run across the street like that," Shiawa scolded her.

"Bah, that is just old-fashioned nonsense. Since when did you give in to this village mentality? And if it was true, I would much rather lose my virginity instead of losing my life, uh." Sahar shivered in exaggeration, laughed, took Shiawa's hand, and led her into the narrow-crowded alleys in the bazaar. Sahar had to buy halva, the sugary sesame sweet, so they went down the passage where the men were selling honey, dried fruit and candies. There was a sour smell, where the Kurdish sheep cheese kept in the stomach of a sheep was on display, but even that belonged to the bazaar. The alleys were dirty with open drains right in the middle of all the lanes. People tried to keep it clean from time to time, but still a lot of trash was lying around. They walked in and out of the rows of the natural sweets dangling from the marquises, and after Sahar had tasted three different kinds of halva, she finally decided on a kilo with walnuts. They went to the tiny shop where the shop owner was selling baby gear imported from Thailand. Shiawa had decided on just buying the best for her baby. She was also thinking about all the money she would soon earn. She bought some white body stockings and some cute little bibs with little teddy bears and a nappy bag. Shiawa tried to look for some maternity clothes, but even though they kept asking for it and were sent into various directions, they never really found anything.

"We can go to the Teirawa bazaar and buy it another day after class," suggested Sahar. Shiawa agreed. She was feeling tired, and they decided to buy a double up falafel and took the food with them to their favourite juice shop and ate the food there with a big glass of pomegranate juice. Sahar had her juice with a pinch of salt, but Shiawa preferred hers without. The TV in the shop was turned on and showed a music video with the Kurdish singer Aziz Weysi singing about apricots, pears and plums while looking at plump village girls. The music was very loud, so they ate in silence and partly watched the video and partly the other few customers in the shop, who also observed them.

It was late when Shiawa arrived in Banaman. Instead of going straight home, she went to the green house and looked at the cucumber plants. Little cucumbers were sticking out all over the vine. She was so grateful that Uncle Ahmed had given her all the natural fertilizers. It clearly made a difference, the workers had told her, and now her plants just looked so healthy. She had decided not to plant herbs this year in order just to focus on the cucumbers, and another thing that she was concerned about was how big the plants would be. Better to get one thing right than getting into a mess. She went along the cucumber rows and touched the plants and tugged in a twig here or a branch there and took a final glance at all her hard work before she went out of the door.

When she came back, Lara and Bahrus had already started eating dinner. Lara had made chickpea soup with curry, and then there were some leftovers from the day before. She greeted them, put down her bags, washed her hands and sat down at the table.

"It is very late. Where were you?" Bahrus asked. "I went to visit my mother. She sends you her regards. After that I went to the bazaar with Sahar," Shiawa said. She knew that Bahrus did not like Sahar because she was very open minded and outgoing, but for her she was a good friend she enjoyed spending time with. Bahrus made it more complicated than it was.

"But you know I don't like you to go out with her. She's not on your level." Bahrus continued. "Did you meet with anybody else?"

"No," Shiawa said.

"But if you feel you have so much time to run around and have fun, maybe it is time to contribute more to the housework," Bahrus added.

Shiawa looked up for a second to see the smirk on Lara's face, but she did not answer and just started to eat the chickpea soup. She did not even care to say that she had gone to the greenhouse to check up on the cucumber plants. He wouldn't bother anyway.

The Blue Donkey

Down the road where Shiawa's mother and uncle lived, construction builders were constantly working on finishing a house for a forty-year-old paediatrician, who was engaged to a young girl from Duhok. Doctor Aram was a clever man since he had always tried to develop himself professionally by traveling to medical conferences all over the world. These journeys had also opened his eyes for other architectural trends and designs of villas, and he liked to implement some of these elements in his new house. The nearly finished house looked to him very elegant and simplistic but rather dull for a Kurdish eye. There were two floors, a huge external chimney built with red bricks, and the facade was covered in white greyish marble. There were still no walls or porches to close, and a donkey had taken the liberty to enjoy the shaded driveway. Architecture was a hobby for him, and now he had fun trying to implement his own design. He had paid a lot of interest in his career and had earned a good fortune, but now it was time for him to settle down and relax. He had bought shares in the new Zheen Hospital on the big One Hundred Meter Road and had decided just to work for a few hours in his private clinic every day and look over his patients in the hospital if needed. Shiawa had met the couple several times when they had come to look at the progress.

One day, when Shiawa came for lunch at her mother's house in between her morning and afternoon classes at university, she saw Uncle Ahmed talking to the paediatrician. Her uncle had gone to school with the doctor's older brother.

"Hello, Doctor Aram," she greeted him.

"Hello, how are you? How is your health?" he responded.

Shiawa's mum had seen Shiawa from the kitchen window and came outside to greet her daughter.

"Hello, Doctor Aram. Please join us for lunch," she greeted.

"No, thank you, mother of Shiawa," Doctor Aram declined. "I am waiting for some trucks to bring bricks and cement for a wall to surround the garden."

"Please join us while you're waiting for the trucks, and when they arrive, we will not stop you from leaving," she suggested." I've made kofta."

"Oh, I love kofta, and in that case, I don't think I can refuse," Doctor Aram said with a smile, and with these words they went inside where Shiawa's mother had set the table, and they all sat down to eat. Doctor Ahmed was talking about all the difficulties involved in building a house.

"I constantly have to argue with the construction builders who generously give their opinion about the design of the house which they, of course, do not like because they've never seen such a design before. They make their own decisions whenever I'm not present, and when I come back, I must force them to destroy what they had just built and rebuild it the way I want it. I am building the house and paying for it, and I'm going to live in it, so I assume it's alright that I decide how it should be, right?" he chuckled. His mobile phone rang. Apparently, it was the truck driver who called and said that he was not able to bring the cement and bricks for the wall till tomorrow morning.

"Look," Doctor Aram said. "I closed my clinic today because I had to be here when the drivers arrive, and last minute they cancel." He sighed.

"Well, then you have time for a cup of tea and some fruit," Najeeba said.

It was a nice lunch and Shiawa suddenly looked at the big clock in the kitchen.

"Oh! It is already three o'clock. I'll be late for my afternoon class," Shiawa said.

"I can take you to the university," Doctor Aram suggested.

"No, thank you, Doctor Aram," Shiawa said, knowing very well what kind of problems she would bring herself into if anybody would see her driving together with another man.

"Don't make yourself tired, my girl," Najeeba said.

"I won't, mother." She kissed her mother on the cheek, quickly grabbed her bag, adjusted her veil and rushed out the door.

A week later, Shiawa visited her mother and Uncle Ahmed again for lunch in between her classes. Bahrus was in Hewler, apparently to sort out some business related to the petrol station. He was a rich man now that he had inherited the K Energy Petrol station with his brother and sisters. They still could not come to terms with how to share all the land, and whenever they met, they started to argue and one of the sisters would start to cry.

Bahrus picked up Shiawa in front of the university and they drove together to Shiawa's mother's house. When they passed Doctor Aram's house, the wall was finished, and a painter was painting it sky blue.

"What an ugly house," Bahrus commented.

"It's not ugly," Shiawa said. "It's just different."

"Only the colour of the wall is ok," he finished the conversation.

Her mother had made roast chicken with rice and beans in tomato sauce and the four of them ate in silence apart from a "Would you please pass me the salad?" and "The chicken tastes really good" until Bahrus was the first one who thanked Najeeba for the food, and got up and washed his hands and face in the bathroom before he went into the living room. Uncle Ahmed and Najeeba exchanged a look Shiawa could not quite decipher.

"Thank you, dear mother. It was a lovely meal." She joined Bahrus in the living room after washing her hands.

"You finished lunch really fast," she said, but he was looking at his mobile phone and did not look at her.

"Hmm?" he said without taking his eyes off the phone. Uncle Ahmed joined them. Soon Najeeba brought tea and fruit. Kak Bahrus drank his tea quickly and looked at his watch.

"Should we leave?" he asked Shiawa.

"Ok," she said. She had just started to peel an orange and kept on peeling it with her little fruit knife.

"It is very early, Kak Bahrus," Najeeba said. "Why don't you stay a little longer?"

"Oh, I have some work to do, Najeeba Xan," he answered politely. "And I have to take Shiawa back to the university first," he said.

He looked at his mobile phone again, stood up, and told Shiawa they were leaving.

"But it is very early for me to go back to the university," Shiawa said. "I'll take a taxi."

"As you like," Bahrus answered.

It was clear that he was in a hurry, and he did not seem to mind. Shiawa stayed back and ate her juicy orange. There were still two hours before her afternoon classes started. She and her mother went to see a neighbour down the road with a tray of food. The neighbours had recently stopped by with dolma, so she had to return the plate with a new dish.

The neighbours' house was just opposite Doctor Aram's house, and now the painter had nearly finished his work painting the blue wall. He had put his bucket of blue paint on top of the wall and stood on a ladder as he finished the painting. When he turned around to take a better look at the passing women, he accidently pushed the paint bucket off the wall, and it landed right on the back of the donkey that usually was standing in the shade of the house. The donkey barely moved, and the worker had to stop that day's work because there wasn't any paint left. He tried to clean the donkey with his old shirt, but he just smeared the paint further into its fur. Shiawa and her mother, who could not help staring at the incident, laughed, but covered their mouth with their free hand.

"What can I do?" The worker looked at them and smiled, raising his arms in despair.

Shiawa and her mum rang the doorbell and the neighbours opened the door. They chatted for a while, and when they returned, the worker and the blue donkey had left the nearly finished wall.

Riding with Doctor Aram

May arrived and the cucumbers were nearly ready to be picked. Shiawa just wanted to wait for five-six more days, and then Bahrus' brother could start to sell the harvest in his shop. It was Wednesday, and Shiawa took the bus to the university in the early morning just to see that her professor had cancelled his classes, so she went straight home to visit her mother before her other classes started at three o'clock. Uncle Ahmed was in his nursery as usual at that time. Since it was still in the day, she and her mother started to make dolma. She called Bahrus and invited him for lunch. She had decided she wanted to cook more for him for a change, and if her mother was by her side, she could help her. Bahrus said he could not come since he had some business to take care of related to the petrol station, but Uncle Ahmed came back for lunch, bringing Doctor Aram – who he had invited on his way back.

"Did you hear about the blue donkey?" Shiawa asked the doctor.

"No?" He looked puzzled.

Shiawa told the story about the blue donkey which made him put his head back and laugh loudly.

"How is your fiancé?" she asked.

"She is fine. She is with her parents in Duhok now, but she will come after the wedding in September," he said. "That's why I have to get everything ready with this house. Hopefully, she will join me to go and buy wallpaper and furniture next time she comes to Hewler because I have absolutely no idea what she likes." He smiled.

"It is a good idea to let her choose," Shiawa agreed. The thought of this happy couple making these plans for their future together made her envious for a moment. It was not because she did not like them to be happy, because she liked Doctor Aram, she could only feel she did not like to hear this comment. It made her think of the way she had rushed into her own marriage and not having had the joy of preparing her future together with Bahrus. She hadn't thought of it then, and now it was too late to redo.

There was a terrible dust storm outside, and Najeeba was worrying about Shiawa's health.

"Stay at home, my girl, it is not good for your health. It is not good for the baby," she said.

"Your mother is right. Pregnant women tend to have high blood pressure, and dust storms can make this condition worse," Doctor Aram said.

"But I cannot miss another class," Shiawa said. "I have already been absent too much."

"I can take you if your mother and uncle agree. Then you don't have to walk up to the road to catch a taxi."

Shiawa looked at Uncle Ahmed who nodded approvingly and said, "Doctor Aram is like a member of our family now." He turned to the doctor and said, "We really appreciate your concern and help."

So, Shiawa accepted his offer and got into his car, and they drove towards the university.

"It is really kind of you, Doctor Aram," Shiawa said. "I am very grateful."

"Don't worry about it," he answered. "As long as you and the baby are fine, we are all happy." He turned towards her and smiled. He was right. Nothing was more important than her little baby, and at this point, she touched her big stomach.

When she got off the bus in Banaman after driving back from the university, she saw Bahrus on the terrace walking back and forth. When he saw her, he stopped and starred at her walking up the hill. She waved, but he did not move, and she got worried that something bad had happened. She hurried.

"Is everything ok?" she asked before she had even reached him. He still did not say anything, but when she was close enough, he pulled her inside, and once they got into the hall, Bahrus pushed her so hard that she fell to the ground and landed on her bottom. She could not speak neither breathe because of the shock.

"What's wrong, what's wrong?" She could see Lara in the kitchen, but she did not react on the turmoil.

"You know very well what is wrong!" he shouted. "You think I don't know what you do when you're in Hewler? You think I am stupid and don't care if my wife is making fun of me behind my back?"

"I did not do anything!" Shiawa said.

"Don't lie!" He kicked her hard on her thigh, and Shiawa put her hands where it hurt.

"Ari called me and told me that you were going out with a man in a big car between classes."

"No, I was having lunch with mum and Uncle Ahmed!" Shiawa cried back.

"Don't lie!" He kicked her hard in her stomach. Shiawa screamed. Lara closed the door to the kitchen.

"You're not being faithful to me," he kept shouting. "I think you need to start thinking about what a good wife is," and then he lost control of himself and kicked her defenceless body in her head, in her stomach, on her arm till she did not move. Bahrus wiped the spit from his mouth and called up Shiawa's mom and put the speaker on and nearly shouted into the mobile.

"Come and get your daughter. She is not feeling well." His voice was shaking from anger.

"But what is wrong with her, Kak Bahrus? Is it the baby? Are you not at home to bring her to the hospital?" Najeeba said.

Bahrus looked at Shiawa and mumbled something.

"But she was just fine, when she left us after lunch today." His mother-in-law said.

"What time did she come to your house?" Bahrus asked and suddenly sat up straight.

"She came right after her morning class, and then Doctor Aram gave her a lift back to the university around three because of the dust storm. He said the dust was not good for the baby."

Bahrus' face turned white.

"Maybe she is feeling better now. Just hang on for a minute." He held the phone in his lap and looked at Shiawa, who did not move. "You know, no need to come, Najeeba Xan. I think she is feeling better now." Then he disconnected the call with shaking fingers, put the mobile in his pocket and threw himself onto the floor next to Shiawa who was still unconscious. He tried to wake her up, but her body was still and even though he started to shake her she did not move.

"Lara, help me!" he shouted.

Lara opened the door and came out of the kitchen. She looked at Shiawa lying on the floor.

"What have you done Kak Bahrus?" Her words were barely a whisper. She looked at him.

"I don't know," he put his hand on his forehead. Together they lifted the motionless body of Shiawa outside and into the car, Lara climbed into the front seat and Bahrus drove as fast as the Mercedes could go. There was a lot of road construction going on and a lot of traffic, which made it difficult both to drive fast and to overtake.

When the three of them arrived at the emergency ward of the hospital, Bahrus carried Shiawa in his arms into the crowded chaos of several car accident victims who entered at the same time as they did. Inside, a burnt woman on a bed wheeled past them, followed by a crowd of weeping women.

"Phew, it smells of barbeque, death, and burnt hair here," Lara said and frowned.

A nurse in the emergency ward found a bed where Bahrus lay down Shiawa. Lara acted as if she really cared about her co-wife and pretended to adjust Shiawa's clothes a little. Her veil had also fallen off, but right now that was not so important. They put Shiawa into a small examination room. A doctor came right away to examine Shiawa, and immediately ordered the nurses to give her oxygen, and they covered her mouth and nose with an oxygen mask. The doctor pulled up Shiawa's sleeves and skirt and inspected her bruised body.

"What happened?" the doctor asked.

"Eh, she fell down the stairs," Bahrus stuttered. "I actually did not see the accident, but I heard the fall, and then I found her at the bottom of the stairs."

The doctor looked at Lara to confirm, but she avoided his look when she answered.

"I was in the kitchen, but I came out when I heard Kak Bahrus call for help," she said.

The doctor put a neck support on Shiawa to keep her dangling head in place. He took her pulse and listened to her heart. He also tried to find the heartbeat of the baby, but he could not find it.

"She is in a coma, but hopefully she will wake up soon," he announced.

Bahrus burst into tears, but the doctor did not seem to care: "I need to know the condition of the baby, so please take her to the basement to have an ultrasound made."

The doctor opened the door and addressed one of the male nurses outside the examination room where women were crying, angry men were yelling, and people were running back and forth. Lara and Bahrus took Shiawa to the elevator to get to the hospital basement. The laboratory in the basement was terribly crowded, and they had to wait for a long time before it was their turn. Bahrus was sitting on a dirty plastic chair in the waiting room with Lara by his side. They did not speak. When the nurse finally called out Shiawa's name, they both stood up, but the nurse held him back and said that only accompanying women were allowed in for this type of ultrasound. Lara followed him into the little dark room. The doctor scanned Shiawa's stomach and after scanning for a while, he said that the baby was stressed.

"It is a dangerous condition, but apart from that, this little baby boy looks very healthy," he said. "Are you her sister?" he asked and turned to her.

"No, I am a relative," Lara said and looked at the screen showing the unborn baby. It was a boy! She thought to herself. Only she knew because Bahrus had been asking Shiawa nearly every day when he would get to know the sex of the baby.

Everybody came to see Shiawa once they found out she was hospitalized. Sahar, Bahrus' mother, his sisters and brother, Doctor Aram and his fiancé, many of her classmates, even her professors and Lara's family paid a visit, and of course her mother and Bahrus who stayed by her side from early morning till late evening. Naturally, Uncle Ahmed also came by to see her every day after working in the nursery. The visitors were kind enough to bring fruit, cake, and bottled water both for the other guests and for Shiawa's little family.

After eight days, Shiawa was still in a coma. The nurse listened to the baby's heartbeat and smiled.

"The baby is fine," she said. "Now we just need your mother to recover."

Lara had not told anybody about the sex of the baby, and even though a lot of the visitors asked Shiawa's mother if she knew whether it was a girl or boy, nobody thought about consulting the doctor who had done the ultrasound.

Back home in Banaman it was getting hot – around thirty degrees Celsius – and the workers in the greenhouse rolled up the green fabric at each end of the greenhouse to make it cooler during the day, but during the night, they would roll it down to keep a steady temperature. Since the purpose of the green house was to keep the plants cooler during summer and warmer during the autumn and early spring, the greenhouse was not made of glass, but of light fabric rolled onto a steel frame. Suddenly, there was no water, and the workers went up to Bahrus' house to tell him to order water. It happened from time to time that they would run out of enough water, and then they would ask Bahrus to call a truck driver to come with a tank of water. Lara opened the door, and the workers informed her about the situation.

"Should we pluck the cucumbers now or wait for Shiawa Xan?" they asked.

"It is probably best to wait for her to tell you what to do," Lara said. "But I will let Kak Bahrus know about the water. Thanks for letting us know."

When Bahrus came home from the hospital that evening and sat down on the sofa and stared into the air, Lara did not dare to tell him and annoy him with extra work, so she did not say anything.

The next morning, Bahrus left early to go to the mosque. He had decided to go and pray and seek guidance from Mullah Yusuf, and after the early prayer he went to speak to him. Mullah Yusuf was quiet when Bahrus told him that he felt responsible that Shiawa had fallen and now was in hospital.

"I did not listen to you at that time, and I did not treat my wives equally," Bahrus said and looked down.

"Ask for forgiveness and don't blame yourself for the accident," Mullah Yusuf said. "Allah is great and whatever happens is His will. Maybe you don't know it now, but there is a meaning behind everything you experience." He paused. "Pray and trust in Allah and everything will be all right."

Bahrus breathed heavily and smiled, and he decided that he wanted to become a better man by stopping playing cards and drinking and treating both his wives well.

He came home and saw that Lara had made breakfast. She had made deep fried bread for him, which he absolutely loved.

"Well done, Lara," he smiled at her, which made her a bit flustered.

"It is nothing Bahrus. If you like it, I will make it for you every day," she said.

"Can you wrap two of them, and then I'll bring one for Najeeba Xan and Inshallah one for Shiawa if she wakes up today," Bahrus said.

Lara's shoulders lowered when he mentioned Shiawa's name.

"Of course, I'll do it now," she said.

Bahrus suddenly hurried and left in his dark green Mercedes to visit Shiawa. He rolled down the window and smoked eagerly on his cigarette, blowing smoke out of the open window.

Lara went over to her parents' house. Apart from Ramia, who was the only working female member of the family, they were all at home. Her mother asked about Shiawa.

"She doesn't seem to be getting any better," Lara said.

"What will happen with the baby if she doesn't wake up?" her sister Roshgar asked.

"I don't know," she said. "Maybe I'll be a mother after all."

She looked at everyone.

"Oh," they all sighed. "Inshallah, Inshallah. God is almighty."

Their brother came into the kitchen and looked into the fridge for a long time before he decided on taking a Coke. He leaned against the kitchen table, opened the Coke, and asked how it was going with Bahrus and Shiawa.

"You know what she had done the day she fell?" She avoided her brother's question by asking a new one because it annoyed her to talk about Shiawa all the time. They all pitied her which made her irritated.

No one answered her. "She was going out with another man. Bahrus found out because his friend Ari called him and told him about it."

"No! Really?" Everybody looked at her.

"Yes, in the name of Allah," she confirmed.

"Who was the man?" Roshgar asked.

"His name is Doctor Aram. And the worst thing is that he is already engaged to someone else. Poor girl. I saw her one day in the hospital when they came to greet Shiawa. You cannot imagine how beautiful she is. Long black hair, perfect features, fair, and small pretty white hands. Everything about her is beautiful. Shiawa just tries to destroy everything to get it all. As if one man isn't enough for her," Lara said.

"Tsk, tsk, tsk how inappropriate!" Roshgar added and wrapped a lock of hair around her finger.

Lara stayed the whole day in her parents' house, so when the workers from the green house for the second time went up to tell Bahrus that they needed water for the cucumbers, nobody was at home to answer the door. They called him, but he didn't pick up. They had been waiting for the water truck the whole day. It was Thursday, and the workers would not come until Saturday. On Fridays, Shiawa and Bahrus would usually go and inspect the green house together and see if anything was needed and water the plants themselves.

"Well, we have done what we could," one of the workers said.

"Indeed, we have." The other answered, and then they both went home.

Scorpions in the Greenhouse

In the hospital, Shiawa slowly opened her eyes.

"She's awake! Thanks to Allah, she is awake," cried Najeeba and kissed her daughter's hand several times.

Bahrus looked at her, but the minute Shiawa tried to focus on Bahrus, pain swept over her face. She was dizzy and could not move, but she looked to the side and saw her mother sitting beside her and started to cry.

"Don't cry my girl, don't cry," Najeeba said. A nurse came in to see Shiawa, and when he saw that she was awake, he ran outside to fetch a doctor. When the doctor came back, he smiled at Shiawa and spoke in a loud, clear voice.

"It is nice to see that you are awake, Shiawa Xan. You have been in a coma, but you are okay, and your baby is also fine." The doctor turned to Bahrus and Najeeba.

"You must observe Shiawa Xan's condition closely. When she is fully awake, we will try to take away the equipment that is measuring her heartbeat, her pulse and ability to breathe. Right now, her situation is stable, and I do not expect anything to happen but just to be on the safe side."

Back in Banaman, the first load of cucumbers in the greenhouse had been ready to pick for a few days. Lara had forgotten everything about it, so the plants simply stopped growing and were at a stage where they were just trying to survive the hot weather. The leaves turned yellow, and a few cucumbers had already fallen off. It was Saturday, and one of the greenhouse workers' uncles passed away, so he had to go and sit in his aunt's house and mourn for three days. Since the other greenhouse worker was the first greenhouse worker's good friend, he wanted to support his friend and also went and mourned the dead aunt. He was just being polite.

Shiawa slowly regained her strength, and two days after she had woken up from the coma, the doctor announced that she was ready to go home. She could not speak to Bahrus about what had happened that day, and Bahrus pretended nothing had happened. Not one moment did he let her be alone with her mother, and he would make sure to take his mother-in-law home and come back early the next morning to pick her up on his way to the hospital. After waiting the whole day for a doctor to sign her medical papers, Shiawa could finally go home. All the way from Hewler, she stared out of the window of the Mercedes.

"Please remember to thank Lara Xan, okay?" Bahrus said.

When she did not reply, he continued:

"Without her help, you would still be lying still on the floor in Banaman. Just remember that," he said and sped up. Shiawa did not know what to think and even less what to say.

Bahrus had beaten her up because she had taken care of their unborn baby. Her uncle and mother had approved her behaviour, and she had done absolutely nothing wrong but sitting next to another man who was at least ten years older than herself. A man who had been considerate enough to offer her a lift as a friendly gesture to her and her family. When she came home, she greeted Lara who came out from the kitchen where she was heating up a soup.

"Thank you," Shiawa said

"It was nothing. Don't worry about it," Lara said and dried her wet hands in her veil.

Shiawa went upstairs to their bedroom. She sat down on her bed and took out her sketch book from the drawer in the furniture beside her bed and looked at her drawings of sheep and cucumber plants. She smiled when she saw her big clumsy drawing of the ram but lit up when she watched the drawings of the cucumber plants' progress from a tiny germinated seed to right before she went into coma. It was still light outside, but the greenhouse workers would probably have gone home by now. She felt weak, but still she decided to go down there to have a look at the plants. When she went downstairs, Bahrus came out from the kitchen where Lara and he were eating soup.

"Where are you going, Shiawa?" he asked.

"To the greenhouse," she said quietly.

"You just came out of the hospital. Stay and relax at home."

"I want to see the plants," she said.

"Ok, just wait, I'll come with you. Just wait till I've finished eating."

"It is ok. I'll go there alone," she sighed heavily.

"All right, as you like. I'll catch up with you later."

She walked very slowly. Her body simply could not hurry. She could not push it to do more than taking tiny turtle steps, and still she nearly fell out of breath. The closer she got to the greenhouse, the faster her steps got. Though the workers would have harvested the first lot of cucumbers now, she could not wait to pick one herself and see whether the harvest was good or not. She pushed the door aside and an awful sight met her. Tired plants that had not been watered for a week, yellow leaves that were falling to the ground, wrinkly cucumbers no longer juicy, and on the dry soil she saw where the new tiny cucumbers on the vine had fallen off. She went around all the plants in the greenhouse and stared at the damage.

"No, no, no," she kept whispering, crying a little, staring in misbelief at her months of hard work now totally damaged. What had happened? Why had the workers not watered the plants? Why had Bahrus not kept an eye on the work in the greenhouse? She sat down on the ground and started to weep. Deep cries from the bottom of her stomach were unleashed.

When Bahrus, a few minutes later, opened the door to the greenhouse, he himself was shocked by the sight.

"What happened?" he asked.

Shiawa just shook her head.

"This is the workers' fault. They haven't done their job properly," Bahrus said.

"Why haven't you looked after my plants?" she looked at him with her eyes smaller than he had ever seen before.

"If it had been your plants in your greenhouse, they would have survived because you would have taken care of it, but when it comes to your wife, you don't care," she said it, and she could feel the heat building up inside her.

"But Shiawa, I was so busy with you in the hospital. I went there early every day even before the doctors and nurses arrived, picked up your mum, took her back and when I came home it was late and the workers had left. Really, the past week has been so stressful for me. You cannot imagine what kind of situation I was in."

She did not reply.

"Shiawa, please say something," Bahrus said but he was still met with silence.

"Your health is more important than cucumbers," he said and then he left her on the ground and went back to the house.

Shiawa was still on the ground and did not notice a scorpion crawl up under her skirt. The heat and the warmer, drier greenhouse had attracted lots of scorpions. When she finally moved to get up, the scorpion got scared and stung her. She screamed from the pain and tried wildly to get it out from her clothes. When it finally dropped to the ground, she tried to stomp on it as hard as she could with her foot, but her legs did not listen to her and it ran away before she could kill it. It was just a small beige scorpion, but still it hurt badly. She pulled up her skirt and looked at where it had stung her. Her big stomach was preventing her from seeing well, but on the back of her leg she could see two tiny red dots. She hit the nearest cucumber plant in a childish way and tried to pull out the dry plant, but the soil was so hard and her strength far from being impressive, so she did not manage to do any harm. The only thing that happened was that a big black scorpion crawled out from under the plant, and with respect for this dangerous species, she decided to give up and go home. It took her ages to walk back. Bahrus was waiting for her on the terrace.

"I called the workers," he started. "They had told Lara about the water problem, but she did not want to bother me when I had more important things to take care of. They also had a funeral the past three days, so they did not know that the damage was this bad. They thought that Lara would have told me about the lack of water. If she had told me, I would have done it, I swear. You must believe me, Shiawa. I've called a truck driver, and he will bring the water first thing in the morning." She stared at him. "Don't worry, many of the plants will quickly recover," he said.

She just shrugged her shoulders and went inside without a word. Lara looked at her as if she was waiting for an explanation or a battle, but Shiawa ignored her, went upstairs with the absolute last energy and strength she had left in her body. She fell onto the bed and slept immediately. Bahrus went into the living room, and soon Lara brought him a cup of tea.

During the early morning hours, Shiawa woke up feeling something wet between her legs. She got out of bed and switched on the lights. At first, she was confused, but then she realised that her water had broken even though she was just five months pregnant. Bahrus was not beside her, but she opened the door and called for him. She called three times from the top of the stairs, and then she heard the door to Lara's room being opened, and Bahrus looked at her in surprise from the hallway.

"I need to go to the hospital," Shiawa said.

When Bahrus looked at her wet skirt and realised it had something to do with the baby, he ran around himself a couple of times trying not to show his panic, went to the toilet, put on some clothes, started the car, came back in, went to the toilet a final time, and lifted her gently into the front seat he had covered with a folded blanket to protect the seat. When they went past Lara's room, she could see the lights from under the door, but the door remained closed, and she was happy that she at least was spared from Lara's sticky eyes.

They went to the maternity hospital on Shoresh Street, but the porch was locked with a big chain lock. Bahrus asked the guard where to enter, but the guard said that no doctors were in the hospital now, and that they had to wait till eight.

"But she needs a doctor now. She is pregnant," Bahrus said. He could not wait two three hours before a doctor would kindly show his presence, so he went back into the car, turned around on the nearly empty Shoresh Street and turned right on the One Hundred Meter road to get to the emergency hospital. He parked the car and ran into the reception. A young male nurse yawned and welcomed him. Bahrus told him about the situation.

"But you have to go to the maternity hospital," the nurse said.

"But it is closed!" Bahrus said.

"What is wrong?" the nurse asked.

"Are you a doctor?" Bahrus cut him off.

"No, but maybe I still know what is wrong, and I have to know if I am going to ask a doctor to help you." He stood up.

Bahrus could not do anything else than explain the situation.

"But that is very normal," the nurse said. "Sometimes the water breaks, and after two-three weeks, the woman gives birth." He looked at Bahrus as if this explanation had settled everything.

"I would like a doctor to examine my wife," he said, and the nurse understood that this man would not leave.

"Ok, I'll see if I can find somebody," and then he left him in the reception while he descended the stairs to the basement. He came back after a long time, still not in a hurry and said: "Sorry, everybody says you have to go to the maternity hospital."

Bahrus and Shiawa had to leave. They had already spent an hour and a half driving around. Shiawa looked pale.

"I'm feeling nauseous." she said.

"Do you want something to drink?" Bahrus asked. She nodded. He drove around in the neighbourhood around the maternity hospital and tried to find an open shop, but it was still too early. An old woman was hosing down the pedestrian walk in front of her house, and Bahrus stopped the car, got out, explained the situation and asked the woman if Shiawa could get a glass of water. The old woman nodded and went inside and came back with a glass of water placed on a little red plastic tray. Shiawa drank the water and leaned her head against the window. She felt so tired. Her husband thanked the woman and got into the car again.

"What should we do now?" he asked Shiawa.

"I need to see a doctor," she said.

"Yes, I know, but nobody is here. We have to wait."

Shiawa closed her eyes.

"I want my mother to come with me," she said, and then Bahrus started the car and went home to Najeeba and Uncle Ahmed.

"Come inside and eat breakfast," Najeeba said. "The birth will probably not start until after several hours anyway."

Shiawa started to weep at the sight of her mother, but her mother just put an arm around her, and told her not to worry.

"I am scared, mum."

"I know, but don't worry my girl."

They ate breakfast in the little kitchen that smelled of strong tea on the stove. So many mornings she had sat here. Her mum had made deep fried bread, and there was fig jam, honey and walnuts as well.

"Go and rest a little," her mother said after the breakfast. Shiawa went into her mother's tiny bedroom where there was accurately room enough for a bed and a small wardrobe. The bedspread was made with old pieces of colourful Kurdish dresses. Her mother helped her to lie down and put some towels on top of the bed. She lay down, but she could not sleep. After not more than a quarter of an hour, she slowly went to the little toilet, and here she noticed she had started to bleed. She came out into the kitchen again where the men had left to let her mom do the tidying up. Her mother looked at her pale face.

"I think we have to go to the hospital now," Najeeba shouted into the direction of the living room, while cleaning the kitchen table and washing her hands at the same time.

Bahrus got up immediately and went outside to start the car. He tried to support Shiawa, but she was already holding on to her mum and did not let him touch her.

They went back to the maternity hospital, and the guard let them in even though it was before eight o'clock. They were waiting in the closed cafeteria, watching the cleaners being busy splashing water onto the floor and sweeping all the germs around the old hospital with dirty mops. It smelled like puke. Finally, a female doctor arrived. She told them to wait till she got dressed. When she got back, she told them that the examination room was being cleaned, so she would just ask Shiawa some questions in the cafeteria. She put a warm hand on Shiawa's thigh and started to ask her questions.

"When are you due?"

"How are you feeling?"

"Can you feel the baby?"

She said that Shiawa needed an injection with antibiotics to protect her and the baby from infections since the water had broken, and she told Shiawa to lie down to put least possible pressure on the baby, which would only make the decrease of water more serious. The water would regain, but Shiawa was already in labour and there was nothing she could do to stop the process. She looked at her watch and said she would try to find a bed as soon as possible. A male nurse went by, and the doctor told him to bring a bed for Shiawa. When the nurse returned and helped Shiawa onto the bed and was about to take her to a room, he told Bahrus that he could not come since it was a maternity hospital and all the patients, and their relatives were women. Najeeba convinced him to go back and stay with Uncle Ahmed, but Bahrus decided to go home to Banaman to water the cucumbers since the truck driver with the water tank was on his way.

"I am doing it for you," he said to Shiawa. "Don't worry." Then he left.

Shiawa was taken into a ward with five other pregnant women who were also in labour. One of them was screaming like a mad woman and made the other women aware of the pain that was awaiting them. Shiawa's bed was put right next to the windows. One of the smaller windows was broken, and a piece of old dirty cloth seemed to have been the temporary solution for a very long time. She and her mother greeted the other women and their relatives who all stared and listened once the mother of a young girl next to Shiawa asked Najeeba about Shiawa.

"It is too early for her to give birth," Najeeba said, "but hopefully Allah will help us and give the baby strength to stay inside her mother's womb."

"Inshallah," the woman said and adjusted her black veil.

"Inshallah," Najeeba repeated. The seriousness of the situation finally dawned for Shiawa, and she felt the fear of losing the baby like a shiver in her stomach. She started to hyperventilate and felt like crying.

"Calm down, my girl. Calm down." Najeeba hushed at her gently and rubbed her arm harder than she intended to.

After a few hours, the doctor returned to the room. The screaming woman was asked to leave her bed and walk into the room next door to give birth, and soon they could all hear her screams intensify in volume. Then it stopped. Shiawa was feeling more nauseous and vomited. Her bleeding had gotten stronger and after the doctor had examined her, she looked at her, and told her that she would have to give birth to the baby.

"No!" Shiawa cried. "It is too early. It is too early."

"There is nothing I can do. Your body has gone into labour and whether you want it or not, you will give birth," the doctor said. "You have to go into the labour room now."

Najeeba helped her daughter into the labour room where Shiawa gave birth to a tiny baby boy. He was alive when he came out. He was a beautiful little thing, white as snow and with skin softer than anything she had ever touched before. He was so little that she could hold him in her hands. She whispered "I love you" into his ear, and then his little immature lungs could not manage any longer, and he took his last little breath in his mother's warm hands. The nurse tried to take the little creature away, but Shiawa would not let him go already. She stared at him and loved him with all the love she would never be able to give him. Till this moment, she had wished for a miracle to happen, but now her tears fell onto the little boy's head. Finally, the nurse managed to take the naked baby away from Shiawa. She washed the little baby in the room's sink and wrapped the body of the tiny baby boy in a white, clean piece of cloth. She also covered the baby's face. Shiawa and Najeeba started to cry and hugged each other. The nurse gave the clean dead baby back to Shiawa and told her that they could leave after two hours if the doctor had examined her. The other women stared at them, and one by one they gathered around them.

Najeeba and Shiawa, holding the little bundle of white cloth wrapped around her little dead son, went out of the hospital where Uncle Ahmed was waiting for them in the car park. They both cried when they saw him. Uncle Ahmed kissed Shiawa on her forehead and Najeeba helped Shiawa into the car. Shiawa refused to call up Bahrus, and she forbade her mum to call him.

"Mum, I am not going back to that house, never in my life."

"Don't say that my girl. Everything will be fine later. Just be patient, my dear. You will get pregnant again before you know it, and everything will change."

"No mum, nothing will change in that house."

When they came home, Shiawa sat down on the couch in the living room. Uncle Ahmed and Najeeba started to talk about whom to call to help in the kitchen and which mullah they should contact.

"As the first thing, we have to call Kak Bahrus, dear Shiawa," Uncle Ahmed said and kept talking about the fact that the mullah would probably be available now if he went there in person.

"He killed our baby," Shiawa whispered, but neither Uncle Ahmed nor Najeeba heard what she said because they kept talking about the arrangements regarding the baby's funeral.

"He killed him," she said, and this time it was loud enough for Uncle Ahmed and Najeeba to stop their conversation.

"What are you saying, my girl?" Najeeba asked.

Then Shiawa could not hold it back any longer, and she burst out with everything lifting the burden of being a second wife. She spoke and cried in between the little nasty stories about how Bahrus had beaten her up the day Doctor Aram had given her a lift, about the damaged cucumber plants, Lara's mean actions, Bahrus' gambling and drinking, and how her husband always would make it sound like Shiawa herself had asked for this misery. That she alone was the cause of the adversity she was facing, and that he was simply a victim in her game. Uncle Ahmed and Najeeba stared at her.

"I don't know what to say," Uncle Ahmed said.

Najeeba started to cry. "Oh, why did we allow her to get married to this man? Why did we not tell you about his first wife? You should have known." She went on and on.

"But why did not you tell us sooner, Shiawa? This is very inappropriate." Uncle Ahmed asked.

"I just wanted to make you happy and be a good loyal wife. I wanted to give him a chance to improve," Shiawa said and took her mother's hand.

"Mum, I made my own decision about getting married to Kak Bahrus, and I should have known him better before I made such a big decision. It is not your fault. It is my own."

Uncle Ahmed called Mullah Yusuf, who made necessary arrangements. Uncle Ahmed called Bahrus and informed him about the sad news. He told him they would drive to Banaman, and that Mullah Yusuf would be coming with them.

They packed up, got into the car and picked up Mullah Yusuf from the Jalil Xiyat's mosque. He was standing right outside one of the beautiful metal porches with beautiful patterns with a Quran under his arm, carefully wrapped in a soft clean cloth. When he entered Uncle Ahmed's pickup, he started to chant suras, and he continued to do this the whole way to Banaman. At the checkpoint, they asked for IDs, but Uncle Ahmed said they had to go to a funeral because his niece's baby had died, and then they let them all pass without asking any further questions. When they arrived at the mosque in Banaman, the men had already gathered there. Shiawa was still holding the baby. Mullah Yusuf conducted the ceremony in a tactful way, and then they went to the graveyard and buried the little baby boy right next to Bahrus' father.

After the funeral, the men stayed in the mosque, and the women gathered in Bahrus' house. Lara's sisters helped in the kitchen and served tea and water. Since the deceased was a new-born baby, they would only mourn together in the house with other people for one day. Everybody tried to cheer up Shiawa, saying that this happened for so many women. She was not alone. She would soon get pregnant again. They all knew somebody who had been in the same situation. Shiawa did not care about smiling politely. She just sat on a pillow on the thick carpet with her head against the wall with her eyes closed. She was still in pain after the birth. When Lara, her sisters, and her mother came into the living room and paid their respect to her, she just nodded a little.

In the evening when the guests had gone home, Bahrus and Uncle Ahmed came back from the mosque. Bahrus had red eyes. He had wanted a child for so many years, and again he felt God was punishing him. He had not only lost his first child. It was also his first son. A son! He put his head in his hands.

"If you had just stayed at home and relaxed after you came back from the hospital," he said to Shiawa. She did not reply or look in his direction.

"If you had just gone home and stayed in bed, we could still have been looking forward to becoming parents," he continued.

Shiawa still did not say anything.

"You don't need to answer me", he said. "You are not answering me because you know all too well that it is your fault."

At this point, Shiawa broke down and started to sob.

"Enough! Just leave her alone now, Kak Bahrus. She has had a very difficult day," Najeeba said. "I think you've done enough."

Bahrus looked at his mother-in-law, but Najeeba had already been upstairs and packed some of Shiawa's belongings, and now she went to get the bag.

"Shiawa will stay with us until she has regained her strength." And with these words, Uncle Ahmed helped Shiawa up, and the three of them left in the pickup.

Home

Shiawa spent many days in her bed in her old room upstairs, staring into the air. From time to time, she could hear visitors and neighbours stop by and then the familiar sound of her mother handling spoons and teacups in the kitchen. Some of them came upstairs in her room to greet her, but she always pretended she was asleep. Doctor Aram also came by one evening with his fiancé and expressed their concern. His fiancé kept looking at her hands with the beautiful manicure and was twisting her engagement diamond ring around her finger. She smiled to Najeeba and Uncle Ahmed at the right times, but apart from that she did not take part in the conversation but only looked at her iPhone and started to check who knows what. Najeeba and Uncle Ahmed told the doctor that Shiawa had been beaten badly by Bahrus, and that this shock had caused her to go into a coma. They told him that Bahrus' first wife, on purpose, had taken part in destroying Shiawa's first harvest in the greenhouse when she was hospitalized, and that this had finally made her lose the baby. Doctor Aram showed his disbelief with a hand over his mouth and told Uncle Ahmed and Najeeba to keep an eye on Shiawa, and if they needed any help, he was at their service. Then the couple left, and Uncle Ahmed and Najeeba were alone in the living room with their empty cups.

"I think I'll go and take a look at the greenhouse tomorrow," Uncle Ahmed said. "I think it'll make Shiawa happy."

The next morning, Uncle Ahmed did not go to his nursery, but went to see how Shiawa's cucumber plants were doing in Banaman. He could see that the plants had been watered some days earlier, but now it was nearly June and the plants needed water every day. He also noticed a few scorpions, which was not a good sign. The greenhouse workers were not there, and the soil in between the rows needed to be cultivated, and they should have pulled out the weeds.

He felt he had to go and say hello to Bahrus even though he secretly hated this man for what he had done to his niece, whom he loved as his own daughter. He went up to the house and sat in the living room with Bahrus. He asked for the greenhouse workers' phone numbers, so he could arrange with them what to do. He did not stay long, and after a quick cup of tea he left.

The following day, Uncle Ahmed repeated his trip to Banaman. This time he did not go to say hello to Bahrus. He had a man who helped him in the nursery, and who could take care of business two days in a row without messing up too much. In his pickup he had a lot of medium-sized lavenders, plastic pipes, and a lot of other plumbing stuff and his toolbox. When he came to the greenhouse, he put on his rubber boots, took the water hose and went right to the middle of the greenhouse. He went back to the entrance and opened the tap and started to water around himself in a small circle. Immediately he saw a scorpion trying to get away from the water. Then he increased the circle and walked his way out to the sides of the greenhouse, trying to get rid of the scorpions inside the greenhouse and to make sure they weren't just hiding in a dry spot. When he carefully had watered the whole area, he got out the lavenders from his pickup and planted them around the edge of the greenhouse to prevent the scorpions from entering. After planting out the flowers, he took the white water pipes from his pickup and started to measure the length and width of the greenhouse. He collected the parts into an irrigation system which he had also done in his nursery. He would have to have a plumber come and do the last part with the electronic watering timer, but now he had set up everything. He went to Masif Sallahadin, which was closest, and picked up a plumber who could fix the rest. It cost him a lot more than in Hewler, but at least he saved the trip back and forth to the city. The plumber worked for only half an hour, and when they tested the irrigation system, it worked perfectly. Uncle Ahmed smiled with great satisfaction and installed it in a way where the plants would be watered every evening. He paid the plumber to take a taxi back to Masif Sallahadin, packed up, and went home.

When he came back, he went straight upstairs to Shiawa's room. She lay on the bed and faced the wall.

"I've installed an irrigation system, so that you don't have to care about if the workers remember to water or not," Uncle Ahmed said.

"Thank you," she whispered. She closed her eyes and let him stand in the doorway in his dirty clothes until he sighed and went downstairs.

The next morning, she stood up and ate breakfast in the kitchen, and even though this was just a small step forward, it was a step.

Weeks passed. May turned into June, and Shiawa was no longer just lying passively in her bed. Her big stomach had disappeared and now it just needed a little toning and then nobody would be able to figure out that she had once been five months pregnant. She stood up in the morning and ate breakfast with her mother after Uncle Ahmed had left to the nursery. Then they cleaned the house and started preparing lunch. Today her mother had prepared rice and beans, and it was ready immediately when Uncle Ahmed returned from the nursery. After lunch, they all went for a little nap, and in the afternoon Uncle Ahmed often returned to the nursery. Daily, Bahrus would call her and ask how she was doing. He sounded really concerned, and Shiawa did not know how she felt towards him any longer. Not hate. Not anything, she decided.

"Shiawa, please come back. You have punished me enough, and people in Banaman have started to say that I have been left by my wife," he said.

"Oh," Shiawa answered.

"But it is ok. All I want is for you to get better even though I'm getting tired of all the comments about being left by my new beautiful wife." He laughed a bit.

"I am fine, but I am not ready for Banaman and to live in the house with Lara Xan."

"It's ok. I'll ask her to go and stay with her parents if this is what you want. Just come back, please Shiawa," he said.

"Are you sure she will accept this?" Shiawa said.

"I am sure she will understand the circumstances," he said, convinced that his second wife would soon return to him.

Shiawa told her mother and Uncle Ahmed that Bahrus was planning on sending Lara away.

"Do you feel ready?" Her mother asked her, already worrying about what could happen to her daughter. In other people's eyes, it was a failure for her to have Shiawa back after such a short time with her new husband. It signalled to everybody that they had chosen the wrong man for her, but on the other hand it was nice to have her back in the house. She did not like Bahrus any longer and felt he was constantly lying and giving Shiawa false expectations. Sahar came by that afternoon and was shocked to hear that Shiawa was even considering returning to Banaman.

"This man hit you when you were pregnant, Shiawa. You nearly died!"

"But I am still married to him, Sahar. I made a promise, and what kind of wife am I if I am not even trying to make it work out after only half a year? I know it will never work if Lara is in the house, but maybe Kak Bahrus will change if I am alone with him."

Sahar shook her head. "I know you won't listen to me but just take care of yourself."

They went out for a little walk when the sun set. They went down the road and looked at Doctor Aram's house. While they were standing there watching the strange house, Doctor Aram parked his Land Cruiser at the other side and stepped out on the road and greeted the girls.

"How are you feeling Shiawa Xan?" he asked. His fiancé was not with him today.

"I am fine, thank you," she answered.

"Do you want to come inside and have a look at the house?" he asked.

Shiawa hesitated, but Sahar immediately said "Yes, please," so she did not have to start a new discussion with her. Inside the house, the workers had just finished laying the dark wooden floor, which Shiawa had never seen before. The walls were white as well as the Moroccan ceilings.

"My fiancé wants wallpaper, and I'm waiting for her to come to Hewler again, so that she can buy it."

In the living room there was a big fireplace, and above was a cage with a little chipmunk that was looking at them, and the girls adored it for a while. There weren't any doors yet, and the bathrooms and the kitchen had not been finished either, but the girls still had a good impression of the place.

"Thank you, Doctor Aram," the girls said, and then Sahar had to rush back home. After she had left, Shiawa went inside her childhood home and sat in her room looking out the window.

Bahrus told Lara to move back to her parents' house for a while to make it easier for him to get Shiawa back.

"She has been through hard times," Bahrus started, "and you have to understand that I am also paying the price because people keep asking when she is returning, and it is very annoying."

"And for how long am I supposed to stay with my family?"

Lara did not like his idea at all. She had not been living with her family for nearly ten years, and even though her marriage was not good, at least it was better to stay away from her parents and experience a little independence.

"Not very long. Don't worry. I'll let you know when you can return."

So, it happened that Lara moved into her parent's house and promised Bahrus not to show her face in the house for at least two weeks.

Then, Shiawa finally decided to move back to Banaman. She dreaded the trip back, but her uncle had told her that it was time for her to move ahead. Before driving up to the house, they went to the greenhouse to have a look at the cucumbers. She had not been there since she discovered the damage, and now she could hardly recognize the greenhouse. Everything looked fresh and green again, and the smell of lavender made her close her eyes for a moment and take a deep breath. The flowers framing her cucumber plants were the most beautiful sight she had ever seen. Shiawa smiled and embraced her uncle hard.

"Thank you, Uncle," she said with her cheek pressed into his shoulder, and he smiled and clapped her on her back. They inspected the cucumbers. After they had started to water the plants again, the plants had bloomed, and now many of them were nearly ready to be harvested.

"Are you ready to take over?" Uncle Ahmed asked and handed her a small cucumber.

"I am ready," she said.

Since she had already missed an exam and a lot of lectures, Shiawa decided to repeat the semester. She was not in a hurry any longer now that Lara had moved out of the house. Bahrus was very kind to her. He helped her in the greenhouse when he was not monitoring the work in the K Energy Petrol Station, and he praised her cooking, which she now took care of since Lara had left her domain in the kitchen. Shiawa was also trying to accept Bahrus' touches, but even though she wanted to accept an arm around her waist or a quick kiss on her cheek, her body alarmed her to move away.

Big Cucumbers

Rabies had inflamed Baji's brain so badly that she died and despite her dead eyes, confusion was written all over face. The weather was hot, and the temperature nearly reached forty degrees. The last bits of green had vanished around the greenhouse, and only near the spring in the village, green trees still stood proud. The Tarin Mountains had been brown and dry for a long time, and all the melting water in Mullah Omar River had dried up. Lara moved into her old room. She told her family that it was only temporarily, but the way they whispered in the corners and sent her worried looks, made her feel they pitied her. It made her angry to see that Shiawa, who thought she was so clever that she could run a greenhouse and sell her cucumbers, just destroyed her life, and she kept thinking about how to get back to Bahrus whatever the price.

An ordinary Thursday afternoon, Lara's Uncle Yusuf came to visit, and both her sisters and parents went into a heavy discussion with Mullah Yusuf about her situation.

"Kak Bahrus is treating his wife very inappropriately."

"We're a sheikh family and feel dishonoured by having to house Lara."

"Yes, it's as if she is no longer Kak Bahrus' responsibility." Mullah Yusuf nodded and listened carefully. Then he asked Lara how she was feeling and for how long Kak Bahrus had asked her to stay.

"I don't know," she lied. She knew Bahrus would change his mind to comfort his own situation, so in a way she did not really know even though he had told her it was only for two weeks.

"I am ok, Uncle Yusuf," Lara started. "But there is something else that I have thought of. It is about the cucumbers in the greenhouse. I have heard that it is haram for a woman to be engaged in this type of work, and I am afraid Shiawa's business will make us all look like sinners."

Mullah Yusuf lifted his bushy eyebrows.

"What do you know about sinful actions? I have been in Holland, and I do know that EU regulations forbid European farmers to sell cucumbers if they were not straight enough. Why this is illegal is beyond my imagination. Is it because the cucumbers are not straight enough?" he enquired.

"Well, yes," Lara said. She had not been thinking about that at all, but it sounded as a good argument. "Yes, they are not straight at all, but it is just not a good business for a woman to be in. Imagine if all the women in Banaman started to spend the entire day in a greenhouse with other men."

"Well, that would not look good at all," Mullah Yusuf agreed. "But Lara, patience is also a virtue. If you're patient, maybe Allah will show you the right path," he added.

And this was his final remark about this case, and nobody wanted to push him any further. Lara was not entirely satisfied with her progress, so when Mullah Yusuf went to say his prayers, she turned to her mother.

"Mum, it is getting late. Tell Uncle Yusuf to stay with us for the night."

"The fox smells rabbits," Lara's mother said. She did not quite understand what Lara was up to, but when Mullah Yusuf returned, she said that they would be delighted if he would stay for dinner.

"There are some religious matters I want to discuss with you if you're not busy".

"Well in that case, I will be delighted to stay." Mullah Yusuf was a man of God, and whenever or whoever wanted to hear his professional opinion, he was happy to guide them.

Ramia started cooking dinner in the kitchen, and Roshgar started to cut up some tomatoes and cucumbers for a salad. When Lara came into the kitchen, she scolded Roshgar for using the cucumbers.

"Don't you understand a thing?" she said and took all the cucumber pieces and flung them into the bin. She also got the other cucumbers in the fridge and in the fruit basket that was standing on the kitchen table.

"We have to show Uncle Yusuf that we don't approve of Shiawa's behaviour, and the best way to do this is by not eating cucumbers," Lara said.

Her sisters simply stared at her, but maybe she had a point they had not thought of, and they knew she would be aggressive if they said anything that would question her intentions.

At dinner, their father looked at the tomato salad with red onions and some sort of dressing.

"What is this?" he asked and pointed at it with a crooked finger.

"It is a salad, Baba. Remember we don't want to approve of women who work with cucumbers," Lara said and scooped up a big spoonful of tomato salad onto her plate. She knew that her father would be too proud to admit that he could not remember.

"Huh?" he just said but did not eat the tomato salad. Everybody else tried the tomato salad, and since it was a recipe Roshgar had seen on the cooking channel Fatafeat, it was quite tasty, and everyone praised it.

"In the name of Allah, this is the best salad I've ever tried!" Lara said loudly.

Mullah Yusuf agreed. "It makes me think of an Italian restaurant in Holland where I once met with another Mullah from Amsterdam. We had Lasagne with this kind of salad." Lara nodded. Mullah Yusuf continued: "In a way, I found it impressive that you all have decided to do what you think is the right thing regarding Bahrus' second wife. Being together with other men in a greenhouse is not at all appropriate behaviour for a married woman."

"Thank you, dear brother," Lara's mum said.

"I have also heard that she has stopped her education to work full time in the greenhouse, is that true?"

"Yes, brother."

Mullah Yusuf did not say more, but he worried about how this story would develop. Despite all, Shiawa had been through some hard experiences, and he looked upon her as a good hardworking woman, but he felt it would not be the right time and place to mention it.

"Would you like some more tomato salad, Uncle Yusuf?" Roshgar interrupted her uncle's thoughts.

"Yes, please," he answered and put some more on his plate.

In the evening, Mullah Yusuf was occupied with reading the Quran and speaking to his sister about her wish to go on a pilgrimage to Mecca. The more the mullah thought about the young woman, all her cucumbers, and male workers in the greenhouse, the more he was convinced that Banaman would be leading a very bad example if she could continue. He was also thinking about his religious career. It would be very embarrassing if he just overlooked it, and he had to figure out how he could present it. He spent a lot of time preparing his Friday sermon and went to bed very late that night.

The next day in Banaman mosque, Bahrus met with his friend, Ari, whose eyes were red from going to bed too late, and he looked less than happy since he had lost a lot of money the night before. Bahrus turned his head away by the smell of alcohol and put a hand on his nose and mouth.

"You should not have come to the mosque if you have been drinking," Bahrus said and poked his friend's stomach with his elbow.

"But everyone will notice if I'm not here," Ari said.

"Yes, but still, it's Haram. If you drink alcohol, you should wait at least two weeks before you start praying again."

"Ok, I won't pray. I'll just pretend then," Ari said.

"It is up to you," Bahrus said.

Both men sat down and waited for Mullah Yusuf to arrive. Bahrus sat on the thick red carpet and rubbed his clean feet. He was thinking of Shiawa. He was so happy to have Shiawa back in the house. Just looking at her beauty and being close to her made him glad, and he realised what a bad influence Lara had had on the atmosphere in the house. Shiawa seemed to be more relaxed than ever, and watching her success in the greenhouse, despite the terrible start, made him feel that he had done something good by giving her the greenhouse. He was pleased to hear that this day's service was about marriage. Mullah Yusuf spoke about the holy matrimony and advised the men in Banaman to look after their wives and make sure their women did not attract other men, for example, by leaving them alone in the company of other men.

"Unfortunately, not all men understand how to treat their wives, and there have been incidents in this very village about women who are being left alone with men who are not their husbands." At this point he stared into Bahrus eyes, and Kak Bahrus nodded.

"There have also been incidents in Banaman where women have not only been alone with men but have also been involved in male business-like male work in a greenhouse." Mullah Yusuf looked away from his papers and the microphone for a moment and looked at his audience, and thankfully they all seemed to understand who he was talking about. Bahrus froze.

"We all have to follow the right path. To walk in a straight line is very important in our community, and we should not accept any indecent female curves. Therefore, we should not accept the behaviour of any woman who is handling sinful objects as crooked cucumbers. These women are committing a sin, and I hereby issue a fatwa that women under no circumstances may touch, eat or be involved in the cucumber business. All men must take this fatwa seriously and make sure their wives follow this religious order, and if they eat a salad with cucumber prepared by a woman, they are eating something unclean and are committing a sin as well." Now, many men sent Bahrus disapproving looks. He was the man who had let his wife behave as she wanted and had led their wives into a wrong direction. They had to suffer the consequences and eat salads without cucumbers.

"This fatwa is such a good idea so we can get Banaman back on the right track." A man right behind Bahrus said louder than necessary.

Bahrus did not try to challenge Mullah Yusuf. A fatwa was a fatwa, and he could not do anything about it. He would have to take over Shiawa's greenhouse again, but now that she was about to begin to harvest, he knew it would make her really upset to hear about Mullah Yusuf's order. Also, he did not really like to work that much. He had money enough from selling petrol, but on the other hand, he could not disappoint her.

When he came home from the mosque, the smell of roast chicken reached him when he entered, and he went straight into the kitchen where he sat down to eat.

He started to shovel food unto his plate. They ate in silence.

"Did you try the cucumber salad?" she said when noticing he did not try it.

"No thank you." he said.

"But it is really nice. It is a Greek recipe." she said.

"Shiawa, Mullah Yusuf says it is Haram for you to work in the greenhouse. Today he issued a fatwa saying that no woman is allowed to touch cucumbers or to be in the cucumber business. He says that I am committing a sin if I eat this cucumber salad you have prepared."

He tried to say it as gentle as possible, but still she dropped her fork onto the plate where it landed with a bang and knocked off a piece of porcelain.

"It doesn't sound sensible. Why would he do that?" She picked up the fork and looked at him.

Bahrus was thinking of something to say and Shiawa continued:

"Is it because you are rich, and the rest of the village envy you? Is it because Lara wants to annoy me? I don't understand." Then she took a deep breath, stood up, and left the kitchen. Bahrus kept eating, and when he finished, he went outside to smoke a cigarette.

Shiawa had gone upstairs to the bedroom. She looked at the furniture she thought was so beautiful on her wedding day, but now it just reminded her of the false façade of everything around her. She tried to take off one of the fake diamond buttons on the cushions, but it was stuck, and she threw the cushion onto the floor. Then she heard Bahrus turn on the engine of his car, and she went downstairs to tidy up the kitchen. She grabbed the bowl with tzatziki and binned it and continued cleaning.

The next morning, Shiawa did not know what to do. She was supposed to go to the greenhouse and pull out weeds and check the irrigation system, but because of the fatwa she could not. She asked if Bahrus would do it, and even though he said he would do it, he turned on the television and started to watch the news. Shiawa was waiting patiently upstairs. She started to organise her books and drawings. When she heard him switch off the television, she thought he was finally on his way to the greenhouse, but then she heard him start the car and leave in the direction of Masif Sallahadin. He did not even care to say where he was going. After an hour and a half, he returned.

"Where were you?" she asked.

"Oh, I just went to buy a packet of cigarettes in Masif Sallahadin. I also stopped by my brother's shop. I asked him if he wanted to buy your cucumbers, but he said that he had not sold a single kilo of cucumbers today. This morning, the mullahs in Masif copied the fatwa, so no one will buy cucumbers any longer."

Shiawa was devastated. "Are you going down to the greenhouse now to check the irrigation system?"

"I'll do it tomorrow, Shiawa. But what is the purpose anyway? You can't sell the cucumbers, so it will just be a waste of water."

"I still would like you to take a look."

"Ok, if this is what you want,"

"It is."

In the following days, Mullah Yusuf's fatwa spread like fire all over Iraqi Kurdistan. Some people took it seriously and others not. In Banaman, everybody kept a close eye on everybody. It was a small community, and people did not approve of anyone who took the slightest interest in cucumbers, and very few vegetable sellers took the risk of buying and displaying the now sinful vegetable. If the vegetable seller had cucumbers, he would hide them in a box behind his counter covered with an old rag, and if the customer was brave enough, he had to ask for whether the vegetable seller was selling *salad vegetables.* Even at the Iranian-Kurdish border, the police no longer accepted pickups filled with Iranian cucumbers.

Checkpoint Action

Since Shiawa had dropped out of university for the rest of the semester, she had not been in Hewler for a while, but this Friday morning she waited for a bus to pick her up from the main road and went to see Uncle Ahmed and her mother. She asked Bahrus if he wanted to join her, but he said he had some important work to do.

"What is this fatwa? We've been eating cucumbers for centuries, and suddenly this man decides it is Haram, just because he has been in Europe, and thinks he is smarter than the rest of us." Shiawa's mother was furious about the fatwa.

Uncle Ahmed shook his head as well.

"What should I do, Uncle?" Shiawa asked.

"I don't know," he said. "What can we do?"

Najeeba sighed, and she stood up and went into the kitchen to prepare lunch. "Should we invite Doctor Aram for lunch?" She shouted from the kitchen.

Even though Doctor Aram's house was not finished inside, he had moved in to get things done, but still a lot of rooms were without furniture.

"Yes, why not," Uncle Ahmed replied. "Maybe he has some good ideas about what to do with Shiawa's cucumbers."

Najeeba cooked chicken, rice, okra in tomato sauce and served it with Kurdish flat bread, herbs, and big slices of tomato and green pepper. There were no cucumbers.

When Doctor Aram arrived, Shiawa was surprised to see that he had lost so much weight. He looked healthier and younger, but also a bit sadder than last time she had seen him. He had brought the chipmunk.

"Hello, hello!" he said.

"Hello, Doctor Aram. Where did you buy this animal?" Najeeba asked.

"Saidawa bazaar. Now I wish I had bought a fox because I initially bought it for my fiancé to keep her company before the wedding, but now she has broken the engagement." He looked defeated.

"But why?" Najeeba asked.

"Well, I suppose it's ok. I didn't love her anyway, and I don't think she loved me, and she did not like the house and the people in the neighbourhood, which made me so mad. How could she say such a thing when you live here?"

"We're sorry to hear this," Uncle Ahmed and Najeeba said.

"Never mind. I thought she was a sweetheart, but she was probably just looking for a rich man to marry who would buy her the jewellery, dresses and mobile phones she desired. Well, anyway, I thought maybe Shiawa would like the chipmunk. Do you?" He looked at Shiawa and handed her the cage.

"Oh, I remember this little one." Shiawa said and looked at the scared animal behind the bars which was partly hidden in its little cave. She remembered the day she and Sahar had seen Doctor Aram's house.

"I didn't really like your fiancé, anyway." Shiawa said and took an old piece of apple away that was stuck in between the bars of the cage.

"We are not the happiest people on earth these days, are we?" he asked Shiawa sarcastically when he finally sat down.

"No, I don't think so," Shiawa said.

"What are you going to do with your cucumbers?" he asked.

"Honestly, I don't know," Shiawa said, and suddenly she could not hold back the tears any longer. She closed her eyes and covered her face.

"Oh no, what did I say?" Doctor Aram picked up a Kleenex from the box on the coffee table and gave it to Shiawa and sat down in the armchair next to her.

"Don't worry. We will come up with a good plan today to make you happy," he said, and then he started to brainstorm a lot of funny ideas about what they could use the cucumbers for.

"We can make cucumber moisturizing cream, cucumber juice, cucumber jam, dried cucumber, cucumber sandwiches, oh no, that might not be such a good idea, ehem…" She opened her eyes and looked at his hairy hand he had placed on the armchair. His hands were big, and his fingers looked long and strong with short and clean nails. She looked at him with tearful eyes.

"No matter what I do, it is considered Haram. If I pick the cucumbers and make moisturizing cream, it is Haram. If I make cucumber jam it is Haram..."

Najeeba entered the living room and said "Cucumber jam, phew! That doesn't sound nice. Why don't you just make pickled cucumbers?"

Doctor Aram returned to the couch.

"But mum, have you totally forgotten that I cannot be involved in any sort of business related to cucumbers?" Shiawa said hopelessly.

"Why don't you just ask Kak Bahrus to do it?" he asked.

"He is reluctant to help me," she said and looked down.

"But why?" Najeeba asked.

"I don't know. He is always afraid about what people think, always has some sort of excuse to justify his actions, and besides, he thinks it's a waste of time."

"Well, I think you should make pickled cucumbers, Shiawa Xan," Doctor Aram said. "After a while, people will forget about the fatwa, or even better, come to their senses and then they will start to eat these healthy cucumbers again, and voila, then you bring out your boxes of pickled cucumbers and make a fortune."

He announced his plan as if it was very straight forward.

"But Doctor Aram," Shiawa said. "If I just put one foot into the greenhouse, people will probably feel they have the right to throw stones at me. Kak Bahrus will never accept it. I am sure of it."

"Well, you did not ask him, did you? And maybe you should not," Doctor Aram replied knowingly.

"He will find out anyway. Imagine anybody who sees a cucumber loaded pickup in front of the greenhouse? They will immediately tell him, and then I'll end up in a coma again." She said this in such a manner that Doctor Aram started to laugh.

Shiawa smiled, and Uncle Ahmed and Najeeba also chuckled. What else could they do but laugh at the whole circus performance?

"If we take the other way to Banaman instead of the main road and go around the greenhouse, we can park the car at the back entrance, and nobody will notice unless it is a shepherd that accidently passes by," Uncle Ahmed said. Shiawa stared at him.

"Do you really mean it?" Shiawa stared at all of them in disbelief.

"Well, we could go there when the shepherd is asleep," suggested Doctor Aram.

"But the dogs will always bark," Shiawa said.

"Yes, and dogs bark the entire night, but it doesn't mean they make you go out your front door to see if there are any cucumber thieves around," Uncle Ahmed said.

"You're absolutely right, Uncle Ahmed," Doctor Aram said. "Well, I think it is a brilliant idea."

"The first thing we need to do is to go and buy some vinegar," Najeeba said.

"No, stop it, all of you!" Shiawa said. "This is not right. I cannot lie to Kak Bahrus. He is my husband."

"You don't need to lie," Doctor Aram said. "Learn from your husband, and you should know that you can let something be untold for your own benefit."

Shiawa looked at him but did not answer.

"Shiawa you don't owe Bahrus anything," Najeeba continued.

"You have worked so hard, and now it is time to harvest," Uncle Ahmed said. Shiawa looked at their faces, and she already felt so nervous that her hands started to shake.

"No, I can't do it," she finally said.

"Ok, we'll do it," Doctor Aram said, and Uncle Ahmed nodded.

Shiawa called Bahrus and said her mother was sick, and that she would stay with her till she was feeling better.

"So, when are you coming back?" Bahrus asked.

"Well, I don't know. When she is feeling better as I said," Shiawa replied.

Bahrus did not protest. Shiawa was the only child in the family, and it was her duty to look after her mother. When he hung up the phone, he was thinking he could not stay home alone all by himself. Who should iron his shirts? Who should cook his lunch? Who should clean the toilet? He called Lara and asked her if she minded coming over.

"Hello, Kak Bahrus," she said in a monotone voice. Since she had left the house, she had been waiting for this call. She asked as gently as possible where Shiawa was.

"Her mum is sick, so she is away for a few days," he said.

She had thought of something more dramatic, but at least she was moving back to her house and her husband. Ha! She could not wait to see Shiawa's face again.

Doctor Aram stayed for afternoon tea, and then he suggested that he and Uncle Ahmed should go out to buy the vinegar because Najeeba and Shiawa would have to do the pickles during the night to avoid a scenario where neighbours would suddenly burst into the kitchen and see two women sitting amongst huge piles of cucumbers. Najeeba and Shiawa went to the Christian area of Ainkawa to buy spices and big plastic containers for the pickled cucumbers. It was still difficult to find an open shop because it was Friday, and they went around for a long time before they found a shop. They bought all the containers available.

"Mum, these are too many. How are we going to carry them all?" Shiawa objected.

"Don't worry," said the shop owner and tied a string around the handles, so they could carry all the plastic containers. He was very happy that he had just sold so many. They did not weigh a thing, but clearly took up a lot of room. They went out of the shop and found a taxi to drive them home. There was no room for the containers in the trunk, so the taxi driver tied the big bundle onto the car's roof, and they were lucky none of the neighbours were out on the street to ask them about what they were going to use all the containers for.

When they came inside, Doctor Aram and Uncle Ahmed had already arrived. Uncle Ahmed had parked the pickup in the garage and closed the porch before they had unloaded the boxes with vinegar. They had brought all the boxes inside the kitchen and were now taking bottles out of the boxes, so they could reuse them to collect the cucumbers later. The kitchen was now so full of plastic containers and five litre bottles of vinegar that it was difficult to move around in there without bumping into each other.

"Doctor Aram, why are you getting yourself into this? You know you don't have to, don't you?" Shiawa said.

Doctor Aram straightened his back and stopped working. He looked at her.

"Yes, I know I don't have to, but as you're probably aware of, there is not much to do in Hewler on a Friday. Besides, I am planning on settling down, so I've quit my government job in Rizgari Hospital, and I only have my private clinic now. Now I just want to start a family even though this might take a little longer than I anticipated since I've just been dumped. Ha!" He smiled. "Another thing is that it has made me really sad to witness what you've experienced, and if there's anything I can do, I am happy to do it." And then he started to unpack another box of vinegar while he said, "And I have never been part of a team who steels cucumbers during the night, and to be honest, it is the most exciting thing I have ever done in my entire life."

They all laughed because this was truly the craziest thing all of them had ever done. Najeeba did not cook dinner that evening because Doctor Aram went to Abu Shahab Restaurant and came back with grilled liver and chicken kebab. There were also Qoshi Shem; big balls of crispy bread stuffed with spicy rice and lots of meat, almonds, raisins, roast potatoes, peas and onions. They were stuffed! After dinner and a cup of tea, Doctor Aram clapped his thighs and stood up.

"Well, I will go home now and change and take a rest," he said.

"I will pick you up at two, and then we have about half an hour to get to Banaman," Uncle Ahmed said.

Najeeba, Uncle Ahmed and Shiawa all sat in the living room and watched a new episode of the Korean series.

"It is so impressive they all know how to speak Kurdish," Najeeba said.

"Mum, please don't tell me that you believe that," Shiawa sighed and tried to explain the concept of voice over, but her mum did not really listen as she was already too focused on what was happening on the screen.

Shiawa felt tired and decided to go upstairs and take a nap. She knew it would be a long night. It was a warm evening, and she turned on the fan in her room before climbing into bed. She could not fall asleep. She knew that the planned action was a sign of a bad marriage. She wished Bahrus had been the one to come up with such a fantastic idea to save her cucumber harvest. She wished she could do exciting projects with her husband instead of her parents and their neighbour. She wanted to call Sahar, but she did not even feel she could tell it to her best friend because she knew Sahar would tell somebody else at a point where she had forgotten she had promised her not to. She yawned, tossed and turned, and eventually fell asleep.

Uncle Ahmed and Doctor Aram met at two and went in the direction of Banaman. The pickup was loaded with the empty boxes and to make sure they would not blow off; Uncle Ahmed had put an old heavy blanket on top of them and tied a rope all over them to keep them in place. When they got to the checkpoint where they were leaving the capital, the guards greeted them in a friendly manner and let them pass without wanting to see any papers. Once they got closer to Banaman, Uncle Ahmed took a right turn and went under the new bridge towards the tunnel and through the mountain to Shaqlawa. The tunnel was not finished yet, but the road was, and apart from Bahrus' house and two or three other houses, no village people would be able to see them in case they were awake and decided to look out the window at the very same time. Both Uncle Ahmed and Doctor Aram got a little nervous once they slowed down and pulled up next to the back entrance of Shiawa's greenhouse. It was a full moon night, and even though Uncle Ahmed had brought a big torch, they thought it would be best if they did not switch it on. Doctor Aram was impressed to see Shiawa's achievement inside the greenhouse. The moonlight shone on the plants, and the smell of lavender immediately hit him.

"What a special niece you have, Uncle Ahmed."

Inside the greenhouse, they started to pick the cucumbers one by one as fast as they could and put them in the boxes, and gradually they loaded the pickup. After a couple of hours, Uncle Ahmed looked at his watch and decided they had to leave if they should make it back to Hewler before dawn. They closed the door of the greenhouse with the last boxes stacked in their hands and drove back towards the capital. Behind the mountains, it was getting lighter, and Uncle Ahmed sped up to at least make it to the check point while it was still dark. They drove in silence. The only sound was of the wheels on the rough roads and the old pickup's motor. A dog ran across the road, and Uncle Ahmed had to steer dangerously away to avoid hitting it. When they reached the checkpoint, the guard stopped them and poked his head inside the pickup.

"Welcome, dear brother," he said to Uncle Ahmed. All the guards were always very polite.

"Who is this?" The peshmerga asked and nodded at Doctor Aram.

"He is a doctor," Uncle Ahmed replied.

"Hm, what do you have in the boxes?" he continued.

"Vinegar," Uncle Ahmed said calmly and stared out of the windscreen.

"Can you please show me?" the guard asked.

"Sure. Old Ahmed got out of the pickup and took off the rope and opened a box for the guard. Doctor Aram bit his thumb inside the pickup. The guard looked inside the box, which did contain six large bottles of vinegar, which Uncle Ahmed had left there in case he would end up in this situation.

"All right, thank you very much. Welcome," the guard said and let them pass. Doctor Aram and Uncle Ahmed took a deep breath and laughed nervously.

Shiawa woke up when she heard the pickup in the garage. Immediately she was awake and ran down the stairs. It was dawn and from all over Hewler she could hear the mullahs chanting verses from the Quran and gently reminding people to do their morning prayers. When she saw the loaded pickup, she put her hands to her face and cried. She wished she would not feel like a criminal, but as a successful agricultural student who was harvesting a very normal vegetable after using a newly imported technique. Information she should have used to write her MA thesis about, but now the dean would probably think it was Haram if she was even writing about this topic.

Shiawa and her mum started to boil the vinegar with pepper, garlic, and bay leaves and cleaned the cucumbers while Doctor Aram and Uncle Ahmed drank a cup of tea. They kept talking about how they had worked in the greenhouse, the guard at the check point, and the dog they had nearly run over on their way back. The small kitchen was full of excitement.

"It is good that I don't have to work before four when my clinic opens," Doctor Aram said. "Because right now I am very tired. I think

I have to go home and sleep." And then he took his keys he had left on the table and stood up. He turned to Uncle Ahmed and said;

"Thank you so much for an amazing evening. I am looking forward to repeating the adventure in a few days' time when we can harvest again". And with a wink of his eye, he said 'goodnight' followed by a 'good morning' and was accompanied to the porch where they all said goodbye to him.

Uncle Ahmed went to bed, and Shiawa and her mum worked fast. The first pots of boiling vinegar were ready to be poured over the cucumbers. Shiawa arranged the clean cucumbers in the plastic containers on the kitchen table, and Najeeba slowly filled them with the spicy vinegar. Shiawa then closed the lid and put the containers into a box on the floor. "Oh mum, it is such a fantastic feeling to see my cucumbers not being wasted," she said.

It took Shiawa and her mum a long time to prepare the cucumbers, and at ten o'clock there were still five boxes of cucumbers left. At that time, they heard somebody bang at the porch. Najeeba looked at Shiawa. The kitchen was a big mess – four large pots of vinegar were boiling on the stove, and a lot of trash was lying around. "What should we do?" her mother whispered.

"Let's just pretend we are not at home," Shiawa whispered back. Whenever she and her mum had not been in the mood for visitors, they would simply pretend they were sleeping or in the bathroom and had not heard anybody knocking. The banging went on, and they held their breath as if the person on the street could hear the slightest movement. Then the banging finally stopped, and they continued the work, but they did not talk for a long time.

Around, lunchtime they had cleaned and pickled all the cucumbers and packed everything neatly away. There were still signs of cucumbers in the garbage bin, and they were afraid just to throw it on the street in case a cat or dog would tear the garbage bags apart and neighbours would notice. They put the garbage in big black sacks and put them in Uncle Ahmed's pickup and put an old blanket on top of it. They heard somebody banging on the door again, and this time Najeeba opened and saw the neighbour standing outside with a plate of little date-filled cakes.

"Hello, welcome, how are you doing?" Najeeba said.

The neighbour took the snip of her scarf up to cover her nose. The vinegar smell was still very strong around the house.

"We are fine, thank you and hope the same for you. How is the family?" the neighbour said.

"Thanks to God, we are all fine."

"I made these cakes. I came by earlier, but nobody seemed to be at home." The neighbour was expecting an explanation to the question.

"Why don't you come in for a cup of tea?" Najeeba offered.

"No thank you, I have to go home and prepare lunch." And after a few more polite sentences, she left.

Uncle Ahmed was still asleep when Shiawa and Najeeba decided to go to bed. Both fell asleep the moment their heads touched the pillow. Soon after they had fallen asleep, Bahrus called Shiawa. "How is your mother doing?" he asked.

"My mum is feeling better today," Shiawa said and avoided answering his direct question.

"So, when are you planning on coming home?" he insisted. He did not pay any attention to her tired voice.

"She is a little bit tired, so I think I'll stay another night if it is not a problem for you," Shiawa added. "I made some pizzas last week. You can just take them out of the freezer and heat them in the oven if you're hungry."

"No, it is not a problem," Bahrus said. "I think I'll go and visit my mother in Masif."

Shiawa hung up and went back to sleep straight away.

In the evening, Doctor Aram stopped by to see the pickled cucumbers. The proud Shiawa led him to the big pantry next to the kitchen where they had stabled the boxes. There was hardly any room left in the pantry. Shiawa leaned against the doorway, but Doctor Aram stepped inside and clapped a box.

"Nice to meet you again, little cucumbers. What an adventure!" He looked back at Shiawa and smiled.

"Do you want a cup of tea?" Shiawa asked and switched off the lights in the pantry.

Doctor Aram could not do anything else than walk out of the pantry and accept. She went back into the kitchen and put the kettle on. She sighed heavily a few times. Doctor Aram waited in the living room with Uncle Ahmed and Najeeba. Najeeba was telling them about how they had refused to open the door and the neighbour who had smelled the vinegar, and Doctor Aram laughed so loudly that Shiawa couldn't help smiling. You couldn't tell that he had just lost his fiancé and the prospect of establishing a family in the nearest future. She brought in the tea.

Shiawa went back to Banaman the following afternoon. She called Bahrus beforehand and told him she was on her way. In the taxi, she leaned back in the seat, closed her eyes, and smiled to herself. Bahrus was not at home when she arrived because the Mercedes was not there. The house looked neat and tidy even though she had not been at home for two days. Had Lara been at home? Or perhaps Bahrus was trying to do his best. She ought to do the same. She knew she had to try harder to make it work. This was their first year together, and nobody had said things were going to be easy. She called Bahrus, and asked him where he was, and he said he was on his way home. She wanted to go down to the greenhouse and watch the cucumbers. In two days' time, they could harvest again, but she was so unsure about whether to repeat the process. She felt she was putting everybody at risk, and if something went wrong, she would be responsible.

When Bahrus came back, she praised him for the clean house. He told her that he had hardly been at home, so he had not been able to make a mess. "I don't like to be here when you are not here." He smiled to her and put his arms around her and kissed her on her forehead. She received the hug and nearly cried. She did not know why, but she felt it had just been such a long time ago that he had hugged her.

"Do you want to go down to the greenhouses?" he asked.

"But what if people see us?" she asked.

"It is ok. It is still our greenhouses, and we grow other vegetables than cucumbers."

"Ok," she said, and went to her room to find her veil and covered her hair. "Is it all right if I bring my sketchbook and make a drawing of the plant?" she asked Bahrus when she came downstairs.

Bahrus mumbled something and she decided to bring it. She needed it for her thesis. This would be her final drawing. When they got down to the greenhouses, they first went into Bahrus' greenhouse and watched the different herbs and vegetables. Shiawa was constantly thinking about her cucumber plants in her greenhouse. After inspecting the different vegetables, they finally stepped inside her greenhouse. Immediately, Shiawa noticed the different atmosphere, and she feared Bahrus would find out everything at this very moment. The door at the back had not been closed properly, and there were fresh footsteps in the moist soil all over. She took out her sketch book and told Bahrus that she wanted to draw the cucumber plant.

"I don't think it is such a good idea," he said.

"But I asked you in the house before we came, so I brought everything with me."

"How long will it take?" he asked.

"Probably about fifteen minutes," she replied. "You can return to the house if you want. I can find my way back."

"There are very few cucumbers," Bahrus suddenly noticed.

"It is God's will," Shiawa said, and suddenly stood up in front of him and tried to make sure he would not go too near the plants and then see where the cucumbers had been plucked.

"You're right, dear Shiawa," Bahrus said and looked around.

"You know what? I'll just take a photo of the plant with my mobile phone, and then I'll make the drawing at home. Then we can walk together. Isn't it better?" Shiawa asked.

"That is a good idea," he agreed, and then Shiawa took a photo with her mobile, and they went home.

Bahrus had asked Lara to go back to her parents again when he found out that Shiawa was returning. He had realised that he preferred to be alone with Shiawa in the house since it made his new wife a lot happier, and he wanted to make her happy – it made him happier.

Lara was furious about being kicked back home after just two days.

"How dare he treat me like a maid that just has to cook and clean for him. What kind of husband is this? He just wants the benefits of having a comfortable home but doesn't want to give me anything in return. I wish I had never married this selfish animal."

Her sisters and her mother listened patiently to the angry Lara but did not know how to comfort her. Ramia put a cup of tea in front of her.

"I don't want your tea!" Lara yelled and pushed the tea glass so roughly away that it fell onto the tiled floor and broke into pieces. Nobody said a word. Lara got up.

"Oh, you don't understand anything. It gives me a headache." And then she went into her room, slammed the door and went to bed.

"Poor Lara," Roshgar said. "Yeah, she is really in a bad situation. What can we do?"

"Be patient and everything will be sorted out," their mother said.

After a week, Uncle Ahmed and Doctor Aram planned another nightly cucumber event in the greenhouse. They would come around two thirty in the morning, and then Shiawa would have to go to Hewler early the following day to help her mum with cleaning and pickling the cucumbers.

"Dear Bahrus, can I take some of the lavender from the greenhouse and take it to our front yard?" Shiawa asked.

"Hm?" Bahrus was lying on the couch checking his mobile phone.

"I want to take some of the lavender from the greenhouse and plant them in front of our house," Shiawa repeated. "They smell really nice. Plus, we will never have scorpions inside the house."

"But we haven't had any this year, I don't think," Bahrus replied.

"Maybe not, but it's best to be on the safe side. Can I?"

"Ok, Shiawa, but I have to walk you down to the greenhouse, so nobody will talk about you."

"Can we do it now?"

"Now?" Bahrus asked.

"Yes, why not? We've finished dinner, and the Korean series doesn't start till eight o'clock. It will be nice to go for a walk with you, and I will just dig up one plant to see if it can survive the change." She tried to make it sound easy in order to convince him.

"Can't we do it tomorrow? I really want to relax after dinner."

"But I want to make some small bags with lavender for my mum, and I am going to visit her and Uncle Ahmed tomorrow." Shiawa was begging now. She had to go to the greenhouse and turn off the irrigation system, so the ground would not be as wet as last time and leave all the footprints. Bahrus sighed and could not think of another argument to stay in the sofa, but that did not prevent him from continuing to complain.

"It is so annoying to move around after dinner. Why do you want to do this right now?" he said and put on his shoes.

"I am sorry, Bahrus," she said, but inside her, her stomach turned.

"All this trouble for plants," he moaned.

"All that trouble" Shiawa thought to herself. She was the one who had had nothing but trouble in her life since she had married this… she did not even know what to call him. She knew bad words, but she never used them. Not even when she was speaking to herself.

When they got down to the greenhouse, Bahrus lit a cigarette outside and waited impatiently for Shiawa to dig up the plant. He did not even offer to help her. Shiawa quickly dug up the plant and put it in the plastic bag she had brought from the house. She left a few lavender branches on the plastic chair and then went to the back of the greenhouse to switch off the irrigation system. When she was at the back Bahrus poked his head inside, and when he saw her fiddling with the irrigation system, he suddenly felt tricked into coming with her.

"Oh, so this is why you wanted to come?" he shouted at her. Shiawa turned around, and her frightened face made him believe he was right.

"So, you want to give the cucumbers extra water, do you?" he said.

"No, Kak Bahrus. I'm switching it off."

He came up to her and looked at the water irrigation system. He had no idea about how it worked, which only made him angrier.

"What is this? This is nothing. Nothing important and you won't need it any longer." And then he kicked the box, so it fell to the ground. Then he gave it another kick to make sure it was completely damaged.

Shiawa screamed. "Why did you have to break it?" She was angry. "It was worth a lot of money. My money!" she said.

"I don't care," Bahrus replied. "Why do you keep bothering about these cucumbers? It was a failure. Nobody wants your cucumbers. They are worth nothing!"

Then he grabbed one plant and pulled it out of the ground and started to stomp on it. The juice from the big fat cucumber splattered over her Kurdish dress. Then he took another plant and did the same. She stared at him in disbelief. He only tried to damage things. He had killed her baby because he had hit her, and now he was damaging her cucumber plants she had spent months on growing. Her two most important accomplishments had been attacked by this liar. She turned on her heel and made a move to leave. Bahrus held her back.

"Where are you going?" he asked.

"I am going home," she answered. "As you said, everything in this greenhouse is worth nothing, so why would I like to stay?" And with her head held high, she went out of the greenhouse and forgot the lavender in the plastic bag.

When she came home, she went upstairs and called her mum. When she told her what had happened, she started to sob. "Mum, I cannot take it any longer. He is just so aggressive and gets annoyed by every little thing I do."

Najeeba hesitated but then said "Come home and stay with us till things are better. Perhaps he will change when people start to eat cucumbers again, and you start to sell your pickled cucumbers. Maybe he will even feel proud you came up with this plan."

Shiawa heard Bahrus enter, and she said goodbye to her mum, not feeling any better. She took out her sketch book and started to draw the final cucumber plant, copying the photo she had taken with her mobile phone. Last night, Bahrus did not come up to her but stayed in the living room and watched television. Shiawa listened to the noise from the T.V. Her hand stopped drawing the cucumbers, but when she realised her mind had started to wander, she got hold of herself and finished the drawing.

Shiawa went downstairs a little before eight to watch the Korean series. She went into the kitchen and brewed a pot of tea and warmed some cakes from the freezer, so they tasted freshly baked. She arranged fruit in a bowl, plates, cups, forks and knives on a tray, and went inside the living room. Kak Bahrus watched her but did not say anything. When the series started, Shiawa poured tea into two cups with sugar, and arranged fruit and a cake on her plate and started to eat and drink. She did not like to behave childish like Lara and not bring Bahrus anything. That would only make things worse. After holding back for a while, Kak Bahrus started to drink his tea and eat a slice of cake. When the series was over, Shiawa took the used plates and cups into the kitchen and started to do the dishes and tidy up. When she heard he got out of the sofa, she thought he might come to her and apologize, but he just went outside to smoke a cigarette. Now there was nothing else for her to do than going to bed.

Doctor Aram and Uncle Ahmed made it to Shiawa's greenhouse at two thirty as planned. They took the same road as last time behind the K Energy petrol station, under the bridge, and then only a few houses in Banaman would be able to see them, and they would probably just think they belonged to the German company who was building the tunnel through the mountain. Since Shiawa had told her mum about what Bahrus had done to the irrigation system, Uncle Ahmed had brought his toolbox.

"Well, I hope I can fix this," Uncle Ahmed said while he was trying to bring the wires together.

"This is really immature behaviour from a grownup man," Doctor Aram said and started picking the cucumbers.

One by one they fell into the box standing next to him. When he had filled his fourth box, Uncle Ahmed had nearly given up on the irrigation system, but he tried for a last time to press the button, and suddenly the water started to spray the plants. Doctor Aram sprang into dry safety while the water splashed onto the box.

"Uncle Ahmed, what are you doing?" he laughed.

"It seems to work. Let's hope it lasts." Uncle Ahmed smiled, and then he installed the correct times when the plants needed water, hurried out to the pickup where he put his toolbox, got a box, and started to pick the cucumbers together with Doctor Aram.

The two men worked until four thirty, and even though they hadn't filled as many boxes as last time, they decided to go back so they could go through the checkpoint before dawn and hopefully without any problems.

"Are we ready for the checkpoint?" Doctor Aram asked.

"Hopefully," Uncle Ahmed said, and sped up.

When they got to the checkpoint three guards were standing there.

"What do you have in the boxes?" one of the guards asked as last time.

"Vinegar," Uncle Ahmed replied.

"Ok. Can I see the papers on the car, please?" He was holding a piece of paper with registration numbers. He checked the papers while he seemed to check the numbers on his own piece of paper with handwritten registration numbers. Then he checked whether the front number plate was the same as the one behind.

"Ok, everything is ok. Just move on." He clapped one of the boxes hard to emphasize his statement. He accidently hammered his hand onto the wet box that experienced the shower in the greenhouse, and it broke open and a handful of cucumbers fell out onto the road. The guards were staring at the cucumbers on the ground, and even though Uncle Ahmed had seen what had happened in his wing mirror, he decided to speed up and leave the gazing men. He had only driven a few meters when one of the guards started to shout behind them, waving to the next guard standing fifty meters ahead. The next guard signalled Uncle Ahmed to stop, but he decided to ignore it. Then the guard took his Kalashnikov gun from his shoulder and fired at the car. The bullet banged into the side of the pickup. Uncle Ahmed stopped the car immediately. Doctor Aram looked at Uncle Ahmed with raised eyebrows. The guards came running up to the pickup and both men got out of the pickup.

"My brother, what are you doing?" one guard addressed Uncle Ahmed. "We asked you to stop."

"I am sorry. I didn't see you. You said we could move on, so I stepped on the speeder. Why did you shoot at me?" Uncle Ahmed asked.

"You said you had vinegar in the boxes, but these cucumbers fell out. Why did you lie?"

"Oh, I'm sorry. I am an old man and I easily forget. I did bring vinegar earlier today. Look at the boxes and the pictures, but these cucumbers are going to be pickled in the vinegar I bought earlier."

"But nobody will eat it," they all said.

"Oh, maybe not now, but later on." Doctor Aram tried to reason with them, but unfortunately it had the absolute opposite effect.

"No," they said. "It is inappropriate. Nobody eats cucumbers these days, and who is going to wash and pickle them?" the guards asked suspiciously. "You know there is the fatwa about cucumbers, don't you?"

"Yes, we know," Uncle Ahmed replied.

"What are we going to do now?" Doctor Aram said.

"Well, I don't think we can let you pass. Please park the car over here," the oldest guard said. Then he went into the office where he called his superior. When he came out from the office he shortly said "Ok, just move on." The other guards started to protest against this obvious misdeed but were waved off by their older colleague.

When Doctor Aram and Uncle Ahmed arrived back home, they were both pale and shocked, and there was no sign of victory this morning. Najeeba saw the bullet hole in the side of the pickup.

"Oh no, what happened? Did Bahrus shoot at you?" she asked.

"No, they shot at us at the checkpoint because some of the cucumbers fell out of a box," Uncle Ahmed said.

"But why did they shoot? A fatwa is not a legal law in Kurdistan. You are not criminals," Najeeba said shocked.

"I panicked and went on even though they asked us to stop," Uncle Ahmed said.

"And I was stupid enough to go into a discussion with them which only made them more irritated," Doctor Aram said.

"Al hamdu li lah, praise Allah, you are both fine," Najeeba said.

"Yes, we are both fine," Uncle Ahmed said.

"But stories like this spread as fast as a dust storm, and sooner or later Shiawa will have to explain all this." Doctor Aram said and both he and Uncle Ahmed tried not to catch Najeeba's eye. None of them liked to say it directly, but they both feared what would happen to Shiawa when Bahrus eventually would find out. Most of the Peshmerga guards at the Hewler check point were young men from Bestora, Banaman's neighboring village and marriages between the two villages were quite common, so it would probably just be a matter of time before the story about shooting on a pickup full of cucumbers coming from outside Hewler would reach Bahrus.

Doctor Aram asked when Shiawa was coming, and when Najeeba said she would come after a couple of hours, he went home straight away. He said he needed to sleep since he had patients to examine in his clinic in the afternoon.

"Thank you for another adventure," he said, and turned to Uncle Ahmed.

"I am so sorry this happened today. It is entirely my fault, and I feel very bad about it. What if the bullet had gone through you?"

"It is over and nothing to worry about now, Kak Ahmed. The most important thing is for Shiawa to stay safe. I'll come over tonight when I return from the hospital, and we can talk to Shiawa about it, and if anything comes up before then, please, don't hesitate to call." Doctor Aram clapped Uncle Ahmed on his shoulder.

"Thank you, Doctor Aram," Najeeba said before the doctor left.

Najeeba and Uncle Ahmed continued to discuss Shiawa's situation.

"How would Bahrus react if he knew what has been going on?" Najeeba asked.

"There is a slight chance that he will never find out, but a good story with a pickup full of cucumbers and people shooting is just too good not to be told and retold," Ahmed answered. "Maybe we should tell Kak Bahrus before he finds out."

"No, it's too dangerous, what if he attacks you? You are not fit enough to end up in a fight with him," she warned her brother.

"I don't know what to do," he sighed. "But I know we should not let Shiawa return to him if her life is in danger."

Shiawa soon arrived and found the grave faces of her uncle and mother in the kitchen where her mother had started to clean the cucumbers.

"What happened?" she asked.

Her uncle told her the whole story.

"You put your life in danger for me," Shiawa said. "Yesterday, Bahrus was in such a bad mood when I tricked him into taking me to the greenhouse, and I'm not sure I would like to experience him being in a worse mood."

"We'll find a solution. I'll go and lock the porch now just in case," Uncle Ahmed said.

Najeeba and Shiawa finished pickling the cucumbers, then Najeeba took a nap on the thick carpet in the living room, and Shiawa went upstairs to her old room. She took a book from an old box in her cupboard, flipped through it, but didn't really know what to do. She sorted out her old clothes and tidied up the whole room. Then she called Bahrus. She needed more time. Her voice was trembling when she told him that she was going to see the doctor during the afternoon, and since it probably would be late, she would stay with her mum and uncle. He did not say much and soon they both hung up.

In the evening, Shiawa was still in her old room now lying on her bed, staring into the old cement ceiling. There were spider webs in the corners. She had to remember to wipe them away. She stared at the brown velvet curtains and the big golden rings holding the thick material, but nothing seemed to give her an answer. She couldn't see a way out of her miserable marriage. This was not what she had been dreaming about. She thought of simply running out of the door and hope a car would run her over and put an end to her misery. She was putting her own family into danger. What if Uncle Ahmed had been hit by the bullet? Or Doctor Aram? He was not even related to her. What would his family say? Her thoughts were disturbed by her mother, who knocked lightly on the door and then came in and sat on her bed.

"Don't blame yourself, dear Shiawa," her mother said, and brushed some locks of hair away from her face.

"Mum, I'm afraid, and it's a weird feeling because at the same time I still like the good and charming Bahrus, but now everything is slipping away, and it makes me sad. I thought I was about to start my own family." She closed her eyes and let them fill up with tears. "I am just a silly girl, a failure who was stupid enough to rush into a marriage without having seen my future husband's home, and without knowing that he was already married. Why do I want to stay with somebody who is not helpful, not concerned about my interests, and not expressing his love through anything else than beating me up whenever I'm not being the perfect example of a wife?" Shiawa wiped her cheeks.

"Don't cry, my girl."

"I don't know what to do, mum. It is a mess." She sat up in bed and her mother hugged her.

"It was also my fault," her mother said. "I should have told you that he was already married. I just wanted you to be happy, but now I can see it wasn't a good idea at all. Uncle Ahmed and I think it would be best to keep you here until we are sure nothing will happen to you."

"But mum, I am afraid he will just come around here. What will happen to us all?" Shiawa shivered from the thought.

"Trust in Allah, and everything will be fine," Najeeba said. "Trust in Allah, my girl." They heard Doctor Aram arrive at the door. He and

Uncle Ahmed spoke with lowered voices in the living room. "Come let's go down my girl. Maybe we will come up with a good solution."

Shiawa wiped her eyes and went downstairs with her mother.

"Were you happy to see the result of today's harvest?" Doctor Aram asked Shiawa.

"Yes, it is great. Thanks a lot for your help," she replied. "I am sorry to hear about what you experienced today, but thanks to Allah, nothing serious happened," she added.

"It was very adventurous," he said and smiled.

They started to discuss what to do with Shiawa.

"Maybe we should go to the police?" Najeeba suggested.

"To do what?" Uncle Ahmed replied. "They will not do anything about it." They sat in silence for a while. Then Najeeba got up and went into the kitchen and put the kettle on.

"What is it that you want, Shiawa Xan?" Doctor Aram asked her directly.

"We support you in whatever you want to do," Uncle Ahmed added to encourage her.

"I just want a happy family," Shiawa said and looked at them.

"But do you realise how dangerous Bahrus is for you?" Uncle Ahmed asked. They were all trying to say things as gently as possible. She had to come up with a solution for her own life. She knew she had to decide, but it was difficult. She didn't like the idea of becoming a divorced woman.

"But it is so shameful to get divorced," Shiawa said. "I don't want to cast shame on my family. I am my mother's only daughter, and I want to make her happy," Shiawa said. "I also want to make you proud, Uncle."

"But don't you want to be happy?" Doctor Aram said.

"Yes, of course I want to be happy," Shiawa said. "Everybody wants to be happy."

"Then I might have an idea," Doctor Aram said and then he got out his mobile phone.

In the evening in Banaman, Lara's father came over for a game of cards, bringing his bottle of whiskey. He brought Lara with him, and immediately she went into the kitchen to fetch ice for her father's alcohol and some salted mixed almonds and kernels. She asked if she could stay overnight, and Bahrus tried to sound kind in front of his father-in-law and said, "Of course Lara Xan, it is your house." Bahrus still didn't drink, so he had asked Lara to make him some fresh pressed juice.

"So where is your second wife, Kak Bahrus? Running around behind your back picking cucumbers?"

Bahrus' ears straightened. "What do you mean?" he said calmly and looked at his cards.

"Haven't you heard about the pickup at the check point loaded with cucumbers?"

"Yeah, I have heard about it." He felt his ears were getting warm.

It was true. He had heard about the pickup, but he had not been very shocked about it. He respected Mullah Yusuf's fatwa, but that didn't mean that he believed that cucumbers were a sign of evil.

"And?" Lara's father was speaking in a very indirect way. "Are you just going to accept this behaviour?"

"What kind of behaviour?" Bahrus asked. "Shiawa has been to the doctor today, and she is staying with her mother and uncle. It is fair enough to allow her a little freedom now and then."

"Are you not suspecting that the cucumbers came from her greenhouse?"

"No, I am not. I was there last night to check whether everything was fine, and the plants were loaded with cucumbers."

"Ok, well. That is good. That is good." And then Lara's father did not say more, but just gulped down his first glass of whiskey.

When Bahrus' father-in-law had gone home after a few games and a couple of drinks, Bahrus slept in the bedroom upstairs and didn't care about Lara downstairs even though he noticed she had not closed the door entirely. He turned off the light and crawled into bed. Lara's father's remark had made him wonder whether there was any truth in the story. He tried to sleep, but he could not fall asleep as he was thinking whether Shiawa and other people were laughing behind his back right now saying he did not have his wife under control.

First thing the next morning, Bahrus went down to the greenhouse. He didn't even eat his breakfast Lara had carefully prepared. He stomped into the greenhouse, and when he saw the naked plants and the repaired irrigation system, fury roared through his mind. He ran back to the house, got into his old Mercedes, and drove speedily into the direction of Hewler.

Shiawa, Uncle Ahmed and Najeeba had breakfast together in the kitchen. Shiawa was still in her old cotton pyjamas; a red t-shirt with the M&Ms patterned trousers her mother had made for her so many years ago. Nobody spoke, but all pretended that breakfast was the most natural thing in the world. Maybe Bahrus would know now, maybe not. Shiawa was dipping her Nawzaji bread into her little bowl of yoghurt and ate some walnuts with honey. She lifted the hot glass of tea to her lips and smelled the cardamom and cinnamon. Uncle Ahmed clapped a lazy fat mosquito between his hands and got up to wash the blood off his hands. When they heard the screeching sound of wheels on the asphalt and the aggressive banging on the porch, they all knew Bahrus had arrived. The banging made Shiawa jump and she burnt her lip on the hot tea and spilled a little. "Run my girl!" her mother said. Shiawa rushed upstairs, put on a cardigan to cover her arms, and quickly wrapped her veil around her. Then she opened the door to the roof. She heard her uncle at the porch and from the roof she could look down into the small front paved yard. She let out a little scream when she saw Bahrus push the door open and smack it into her uncle's face and caused him to bump into the wall. Her hands trembled when she closed the old metal door with a big rock, went under the cloth lines and jumped to the neighbour's roof. She jumped the small space between the houses on the road and ran across the neighbours' roofs until she came to Doctor Aram's house down the road. She jumped onto his roof and started crawling down an external waterspout. Halfway down, she nearly lost her grip when one of her plastic flip flops fell off. She held on tight to the waterspout for a moment. Then she just sprang and landed in the garden and ran around the house to Doctor Aram's back door and rang the bell breathing heavily until she heard rushing steps behind the door. She stared at the beautifully carved wooden door until it opened.

"Bahrus is here!" she exclaimed. He quickly pulled her inside, shut the door, and turned the key several times to make sure it was locked. When he turned around and saw Shiawa's hands were shaking, he gently laid an arm around her.

"It's ok. It's ok, Shiawa. You are safe," Doctor Aram said. They were standing like this until awkwardness separated them.

"I blamed myself so much for what for you experienced that day because I wasn't careful enough. I should at least have considered the possibility of an angry husband showing up at some point," Doctor Aram said.

"No, it can never be your fault and neither mine," Shiawa answered. "Bahrus is an unfair husband, and even if I made a mistake, it didn't give him the right to beat me," she said.

"We have to go to a lawyer, Shiawa. You must get a divorce as soon as possible," Doctor Aram said.

"But I am not dressed properly," Shiawa answered.

"Don't worry. We can stop in Teirawa and buy an abbaiya for you to put over your pyjamas." he said.

Out on the road, Shiawa heard Bahrus yelling in the distance and she saw a crowd of neighbours had gathered outside her mum and Uncle Ahmed's house. A police car was approaching. Her mum had probably called for help. She flung open the door and threw herself on the floor of the Land Cruiser and Doctor Aram threw a blanket over her and started the car and off they went.

"Shiawa, we're in Teirawa now. I'll park here and be back in a minute. Just wait." Shiawa did not move under the blanket while Doctor Aram ran into the small lanes in the bazaar and stopped at the first shop who sold the black abbaiyas. A policeman was walking into the direction of the illegally parked Land Cruiser. He stopped in front of the big vehicle and was taking out his notebook when Doctor Aram returned with the black clothes in a plastic bag. "Wait kaka, wait. I am leaving now," he said to the policeman. "You are not allowed to park her," the policeman said. "Yes, I know, and I will leave now. It was an emergency." The policeman let him go. He had not written down the registration number anyway.

They took off fast. Shiawa took the blanket off and tried to get the abbaiya on while they were driving. As soon as she was wearing the decent garments, she crawled into the passenger seat. Doctor Aram glanced at her.

"Very nice," he said.

"I am sure," she answered with sarcasm.

Close to the citadel, they stopped in front of a small office that belonged to one of Doctor Aram's friends. He was a lawyer and a specialist in marital matters. They went inside and Doctor Aram introduced her after greeting his friend.

"Shiawa this is a lawyer I spoke to last night about your situation. Do you want to tell him your story?"

Shiawa told the lawyer that she had been tricked into marrying Bahrus without knowing he was already married to another woman. When she explained that he had taken her to Makhmoor to sign the marital contract, he interrupted her.

"Oh yes, that sounds very typical for these kind of men."

Shiawa told the lawyer how she had ended up in a coma after Bahrus had beaten her, and how she had lost the baby when he had not taken proper care of her greenhouse when she was in hospital. The lawyer was noting down something in his notebook while his assistant brought them two bottles of water and two glasses of tea.

"You have a strong case, Shiawa Xan," he finally said. "In Kurdistan region of Iraq, it is against the law to marry two wives unless the first wife accepts the second wife, and it means that Bahrus' first wife should have come to court and signed these papers that would show her content. To avoid involving his first wife into this, he took you outside Kurdistan region and had you sign the marital contract in Makhmoor. Physical violence against women is also illegal, and since you have been in a coma and lost your unborn baby, the judge will most likely be willing to grant you the divorce even though Bahrus might object, and since you don't have any children, he might even decide to say the marriage never existed because it was never legal in the first place. What you need to do now, is to go to the police station and tell them about this offense. I am writing a note for them, so they understand what law Bahrus is breaking."

Then the lawyer handed Doctor Aram the note, stood up, and said goodbye, and Shiawa and Doctor Aram went to the nearest police station.

The police station was a typical two-story governmental building built in the communist style with lots of cement and many small windows. Doctor Aram and Shiawa stood at the counter and waited for somebody to serve them. A little dirty boy wearing cheap white plastic shoes with red and blue shoelaces sat on a chair in the waiting room, but apart from that nobody else was there. A police officer was chatting with someone on Facebook and didn't seem to pay attention to them.

"Excuse me," Doctor Aram said. "We are here to report a crime."

The police officer looked up shortly but didn't seem to pay attention to anything else than the computer. He shifted from one side to the other on his chair for another minute and quickly typed something and finally stood up.

"Welcome," he said and waited for them to present their case.

"We are here to report a crime," Doctor Aram said.

"About what?" The police officer heard a new chat message was ticking in and turned around and bent down to check it on his computer.

"It is about a man who has married two wives," Doctor Aram started.

"But it is not a problem. I know a man, and he has two wives. He has a room in the middle of his house and on each side of his room his wives have their rooms, and they are all living happily together. It is not a crime." He turned to Shiawa and asked her: "Are you the wife?"

"Yes," Shiawa said.

"And you don't want to be married to your husband any longer?"

"That is correct," Shiawa said.

"But it is Haram to get divorced," he said and looked up at Shiawa. "For how long have you been married?"

"Please, just give us the form." Doctor Aram interrupted the conversation and showed him the note from the lawyer which explained the legal issues.

"As you like." The police officer read the note and grunted and gave them a form to fill in.

Doctor Aram and Shiawa sat down in the waiting room together with the dirty boy, and Doctor Aram filled in the form for Shiawa.

"What are you doing here?" Shiawa asked the little boy.

"They took my things," he said.

"What things?" Shiawa asked.

"I was selling razor blades and shoelaces, but they said I couldn't sell it, so they took it all. I tried to run away, but they caught me and took me here because they say it is illegal for children to sell things. Some of my friends went to our centre to say what happened and now the manager is trying to get my things back."

He said the last bit with pride, and Shiawa was certain he would be ok.

"Oh, I am sorry to hear that," she said and smiled. "I am sure he will get your things back. Don't worry."

"Good," the little boy answered with a little smile.

Doctor Aram asked Shiawa to sign the form, and then he got up and handed the police officer the form. He glanced at it, and then stamped it with two different stamps and told them to go to the next office. In the next office, two other police officers looked at the paper, and then one of them lifted the telephone and called somebody to pick up an arrest order. Then he himself completed a form which the other man stamped. A fourth police officer appeared and took the arrest order and addressed Doctor Aram.

"Where can we find this Bahrus, so we can arrest him?"

"We can lead you to him," Doctor Aram said, and then the three of them left the station. The police officer went to the parking lot and went into the driver's unit to get a policeman to drive the police car and followed Doctor Aram's Land Cruiser back to Najeeba and Uncle Ahmed's house where Bahrus was still waiting for Shiawa to show up.

When the two police officers stood outside Najeeba's and Uncle Ahmed's house, Shiawa and Doctor Aram stayed in the Land Cruiser further down the road. There was no need to escalate the situation by showing up together with the police. Soon the police officers were leading Bahrus out in hand cuffs. All the neighbours starred at Bahrus. When the police turned the car around and went back into the direction of the police station, the neighbours gathered around Uncle Ahmed and Najeeba and started asking lots of questions. Shiawa and Doctor Aram walked up to all of them. Shiawa found her mum and hugged her. She cried into her shoulder. "It is over now, my girl," her mother said. "It is over now."

Bahrus was taken to the prison next to the university in Hewler where he waited for the judge's decision. They put him in chains and took him into the building that had once been a railway station. The heavy metal door closed with a tired creaking, and he sat down on his bunk bed with all the other prisoners looking at him, waiting for him to tell his story. "Have you not heard about the law about polygamy?" one of the prisoners said when Bahrus had finished the story. "Yes, but I got married with my second wife in Makhmoor to protect my first wife, and I never ever imagined it would actually have any consequences for me. . ."

"I am also innocent," one of the prisoners said. "It is the government's fault. The people are not ready for all these changes. It is absurd that you are in prison." The other prisoners nodded in silence.

"I wished I had never remarried," Bahrus said. "This woman is an evil person, and I never want to see her again. She has brought so many problems to my village."

"We will pray for you," one of the men said.

"Thank you, brothers. Allah is great." Bahrus said.

New Furniture

Shiawa moved in with her mother and Uncle Ahmed. Uncle Ahmed managed to sell Shiawa's land and the greenhouse in Banaman to somebody in Masif, and the deal made Shiawa richer than she had ever imagined. Soon everybody also started to eat cucumbers again, and Shiawa managed to get a deal with Kook Supermarket that started to sell her pickled cucumbers. Doctor Aram had the blue wall painted white, but he still hadn't furnished many of the rooms in his big house. From time to time, Shiawa brought him a tray of food, or he would come to their house for lunch. They were all waiting for the verdict.

Nearly five months after Bahrus' arrest, the lawyer finally called Doctor Aram in his clinic.

"The court has decided that Shiawa's marriage was an annulment," he told Doctor Aram.

"Really?" Doctor Aram asked.

"In the name of Allah, yes," the lawyer repeated. "Bahrus has been sentenced to two years in prison."

"Oh, that is happy news. I'll tell Shiawa tonight," Doctor Aram said. He thanked his friend and hung up.

In the evening, Doctor Aram came over unannounced with a kilo of sweet Baklava from Ashtar's bakery. He looked handsome and very excited, Shiawa noticed. When they were all gathered in the living room sipping their tea and tasting the crunchy cakes, Doctor Aram started to speak:

"I have an announcement," he started. "The lawyer called me today, and I would like to inform you that the judge of Hewler has decided that Shiawa's marriage to Bahrus was illegal and never existed."

"Oh!" Najeeba and Shiawa screamed and hugged each other. Uncle Ahmed just looked really happy.

"Oh, mum, let's go for a drive to celebrate!" Shiawa said excitedly.

"Shiawa dear, it is late." Najeeba looked at her watch.

"Oh, please mum." She looked at Uncle Ahmed, but it was Doctor Aram who helped her.

"I can take you around the city if you like and if your mum and uncle approve," he said and looked at Najeeba and Uncle Ahmed. They looked a bit surprised. Doctor Aram was too old to take out their daughter.

"Mum, please," Shiawa said and then both Uncle Ahmed and Najeeba nodded. It would not be polite to refuse.

Shiawa ran upstairs to get dressed. They all walked down to Doctor Aram's house where Shiawa and Doctor Aram got into his Land Cruiser. Uncle Ahmed and Najeeba waved goodbye.

First, they went to 'Café Me and You' where they had a pistachio ice cream. As they sat down, his elbow accidently touched Shiawa's arm, but she pretended nothing had happened.

Doctor Aram suddenly pointed across the street.

"Look!" he said. Opposite the ice cream bar, the blue donkey was standing outside a furniture shop.

"It must be a sign," Shiawa laughed.

"What do you mean?" He looked puzzled.

"Well, maybe you need to buy some furniture for your new house," Shiawa said.

"You are right," he said. "It is time to move on."

"Great! I have never tried to shop for furniture, and I would love to help you after all you have done for me," Shiawa said.

"All right let's go and buy some furniture for my home," he said and stood up. He paid for the ice creams, and then they crossed the busy road and went into the furniture shop.

- The End -

Glossary

Abbaiya: A long garment (usually black) worn by some Muslim women
Al hamdu li lah: An expression meaning 'Thanks to Allah'
Baji: A polite title often used for older women
Fatwa: A religious decision made by an Islamic scholar
Haram: An Islamic term referring to what is forbidden
Inshallah: An Islamic expression meaning 'If Allah wills it'
Kak/Kaka: A polite title used for men
Mashallah: A term meaning 'as Allah willed' and used to wish for Allah's protection from the evil eye e.g. if a girl is very beautiful
Mullah: A person conducting religious ceremonies in a mosque
Peshmerga: Kurdish soldier
Salaam Aleikum: A greeting used by Muslims meaning 'Peace be upon you'
Serupe: A traditional dish with the head and feet of a sheep
Sura: A chapter of the Quran
Xan: A polite title used for especially married women

Acknowledgements

First, I want to thank Christina Taheri for her amazing support while writing and editing this book. Her encouragement and feedback kept me going to the last full stop.

Big thanks also go to Mette Bendixen Jensen, Hope Kakarash, Nina Bro, Judith Beamont, Gabrielle Airey, Kirstin Crawford, Sozan Kadir and Shayma Qader Kamala for valuable feedback and proofreading.

I would also like to thank my sister in law Suzan Sheikh Reza Goulani, who once told me the Kurdish tale about the blue donkey. She heard the story from my father in law, who used to refer to the blue donkey, whenever the same person or problem was being discussed repeatedly.

I also owe big thanks to the village Banaman that inspired me daily when I drove past it on my way to work. I do not know any villagers in Banaman, and the plot is a pure product of my imagination.

Polygamy is illegal in the Kurdistan Region of Iraq. However, it is legal in the rest of Iraq. I have met first and seconds wives, and I have met children who have told me they had two mothers. I have also met men who had a second wife or wanted a second wife. It is hard for me to believe that it is problem free to share a husband, and the idea has been a great inspiration for me. All my thoughts go to these families.

A lot of what I have written in this book is based on what I have seen and heard in Kurdistan, so I am in eternal debt to all the people in Kurdistan I have met on my way and who have given me enough material to write this book. Despite the massive inspiration, no characters in the book reflect real people or events and any resemblance is purely coincidental.

Finally, but not least, I want to thank the kind Kurdish gentleman Safin Sheikh Reza Goulani whose name is written in my wedding ring.

www.ingramcontent.com/pod-product-compliance
Ingram Content Group UK Ltd.
Pitfield, Milton Keynes, MK11 3LW, UK
UKHW022029190726
13853UKWH00005B/2180